Greatest Teams

The most dominant powerhouses in sports

Greatest Teams

THE MOST DOMINANT POWERHOUSES IN SPORTS

by Tim Crothers

ISBN 1-883013-28-3
Manufactured in the United States of America
First printing 1998

Sports Illustrated Director of Development: STANLEY WEIL

GREATEST TEAMS
Project Director: MORIN BISHOP
   Senior Editors: JOHN BOLSTER, SALLY GUARD, EVE PETERSON
   Reporters: DANA GELIN, LAUREN CARDONSKY, JESSICA GOLDSTEIN
   Photography Editors: JOHN S. BLACKMAR, TED MENZIES
Designers: BARBARA CHILENSKAS, JIA BAEK

GREATEST TEAMS was prepared by
Bishop Books, Inc.
611 Broadway
New York, New York 10012

Cover photograph:
JOHN BIEVER

TIME INC. HOME ENTERTAINMENT
Managing Director: DAVID GITOW
Director, Continuities and Single Sales: DAVID ARFINE
Director, Continuities and Retention: MICHAEL BARRETT
Director, New Products: ALICIA LONGOBARDO
Product Managers: CHRISTOPHER BERZOLLA, ROBERT FOX, STACY
HIRSCHBERG, MICHAEL HOLAHAN, AMY JACOBSSON, JENNIFER
MCLYMAN, DAN MELORE
Manager, Retail and New Markets: THOMAS MIFSUD
Associate Product Managers: LOUISA BARTLE, ALISON EHRMANN,
NANCY LONDON, DAWN WELAND
Assistant Product Managers: MEREDITH SHELLEY, BETTY SU
Editorial Operations Director: JOHN CALVANO
Fulfillment Director: MICHELLE GUDEMA
Financial Director: TRICIA GRIFFIN
Associate Financial Manager: AMY MASELLI
Marketing Assistant: SARAH HOLMES

CONSUMER MARKETING DIVISION
Production Director: JOHN E. TIGHE
Book Production Manager: DONNA MIANO-FERRARA
Assistant Book Production Manager: JESSICA MCGRATH

Special thanks to: JOSEPH NAPOLITANO

Contents

Pythagoras didn't leave behind a theorem for this one. There is no mathematical equation to determine which are the greatest teams in the history of sports. There is no Ph.D. on the subject. Not even a credible video game. So I must begin this book with a disclaimer. I have absolutely no idea which are the 30 greatest teams in history, and I have as good an idea as anybody else. I have no clue in what order they should be listed, but I am the closest thing to an expert that there is on this planet.

Therein lies the fun of this book. Everyone's

Cousy (left) and his Celtics had seven teams to contend with; Jordan (above) and his Bulls had 28. Is it any wonder recent teams tend to get the nod on our list?

passion for sports is fueled by wanton debate. Even more so, it seems, when there is clearly no right or wrong answer. Sure, I realize that comparing the Brooklyn Dodgers of the 1950s to the Los Angeles Dodgers of the 1960s is like comparing apples to oranges. Heck, analyzing those same Brooklyn Dodgers against the New York Islanders of the '80s is like comparing apples to motor oil.

So what are my criteria? How exactly do I define *greatness*? Gut feeling. I started with a pool of around 40 stellar teams and then erased them one by one until only 30 remained. My decisions were ethereal, brutally subjective and ultimately personal. Once I had the 30 finalists I counted the rings. First, I separated the dynasties into their own pantheon. Then I discovered that I could segregate another group of teams into a fraternity of champions which had dominated an entire decade.

Ordering the teams within each section was the toughest task. I tinkered with my list based on how challenging it was for each team to dominate its particular era and the enduring impact

each team had on the sporting landscape, and I gave extra credit to teams that had one season that stood out as being among the best in history. You will notice that in most cases I have favored contemporary teams over their predecessors. This approach has nothing to do with the age-old argument that Michael Jordan would dribble circles around George Mikan. I simply believe it has become increasingly difficult to win consistently in recent years. While some fans argue that expansion has diluted talent and made winning easier, I think more teams mean more competi-

tion and more rounds of playoffs, which offer more chances to get sidetracked along the road to a title. For instance, the 1955 Detroit Red Wings endeavored to be the best in a six-team league, while today's Red Wings must be the best among 26. In '55 the Red Wings had to survive two rounds of playoffs. Today there are four.

I have attempted to defend my most controversial decisions in the introductions to each chapter. Inevitably there will be dissension. Rant and rave as long as you wish. And, hey, if you really don't like my picks, write your own book.

Comparing a baseball team such as the A's of Bert Campaneris (left) to the Islanders hockey squad of Billy Smith (below) may be like comparing apples to motor oil, but the author took on the task anyway. Result: A's No. 14, Islanders No. 15.

Dynasties

Dynasties

Argue all you will, but has there ever been a team blessed with three icons of the magnitude of Mickey Mantle (left), Babe Ruth (right) and Lou Gehrig (far right)?

What is a dynasty? A franchise that everybody loves to hate. Poll baseball fans around the country about which team they most enjoy watching go down to defeat and the New York Yankees win in a landslide. Same goes for basketball fans and the Boston Celtics. Every hockey fan outside of Quebec revels in misfortune suffered by the mighty Montreal Canadiens. This near-universal loathing is the ultimate goal of every sports franchise.

How to get hated? Win too much. The Montreal Canadiens have won 24 Stanley Cups. The New York Yankees have won 23 World Series. The Boston Celtics have won 16 NBA titles. No other team in the NBA, NFL, NHL or Major League Baseball has won more than 11 championships.

Therefore, these three teams are the true dynasties in sports.

I had originally intended to divide these dynasty teams into subsets of several years, as I did with the other teams in the book. But as it happens, for instance, Montreal's Stanley Cup teams of Maurice Richard blend into those of Jacques Plante, which mingle with those of Jean Beliveau and Henri Richard and Ken Dryden, and so on, until there is no place to break and begin again. These dynasties are a conglomeration of so many remarkable seasons that they simply can't be divided into brief eras, but must be viewed as a whole.

Appreciate these dynasties, for we will never see their like again. Over the years, sport has

15

The Canadiens of Ken Dryden (in goal, left) seemed to flow without interruption from the legendary Habs teams of yore; the personal title run of Russell (left) may be the most impressive of all: 13 seasons, 11 NBA championships.

legislated against the genre. It is virtually impossible to dominate longterm under the current restrictions, which include free agency, salary caps and an amateur draft which works to create sport socialism by letting the worst teams choose first. Check out the numbers. Our three dynasties have won a combined 63 league championships, but their success has dropped off gradually in each decade since the 1960s and they have combined for just two of those titles in the '90s.

I labored to determine a pecking order for these three great teams. Finally, I put the Yankees on top because they are sport's original dynasty. The team had won its first 10 World Series titles before either the Celtics or the Canadiens even began to distinguish themselves. The Yankees are the Team of the Century, the standard by which all other franchises are measured.

I placed the Celtics above the Canadiens because in their early years the Celtics competed on a more level playing field. Despite the Canadiens' preference for players from Quebec, Montreal general manager Frank Selke's farm system still accessed 750 teams from Nova Scotia to British Columbia, a feeder system bigger than all of the other NHL clubs combined. The Celtics, meanwhile, had to acquire most of their talent through the NBA draft, like every other team, which makes their success just slightly more impressive.

There's no question that rating dynasties is a haven for second guessers. I'd like to see a Chinese historian rank the Hsia Dynasty against the Ming and the Ch'ing. Suffice it to say, they were all pretty grand and they all lasted a very long time.

1

The New York Yankees are the CEOs of American sports, dressed appropriately in pinstripe suits. They are the dynasty of all dynasties. The Bronx Bombers have ascended to heights that no other franchise in baseball can even approach. They have won an astonishing 23 World Series titles—far more than twice the total championships of any other major league team—and 34 American League pennants. After winning the 1939 World Series the Yankees were the only big league team ever to win four straight titles ... until they topped that record by capturing five straight from '49 to '53. One of the Yankees' Hall of Fame players, Whitey Ford, is even nicknamed "The Chairman of the Board."

Throughout the history of baseball, Yankee greatness has been positively relentless. They won their first World Series title in '23, and went on to win at least one—and usually lots more—in the '30s, '40s, '50s, '60s, '70s and '90s. During their most glorious

Two Yankee titans: Gehrig, who played in 2,130 straight games before benching himself in 1939 (left), and Ruth (right), the original Sultan of Swat.

Spotlight

He was this century's first player to hit four home runs in a single game. His record of 23 career grand slams still stands. In the 1928 World Series against the Cardinals, he hit a whopping .545. In 1934 he won the Triple Crown by batting .363 with 49 home runs and 165 RBI. That same year he had 18 more homers than strikeouts. Yet, because he shared the dugout with Babe Ruth and then Joe DiMaggio, Henry Louis Gehrig's accomplishments were often overshadowed.

If ever Gehrig deserved the limelight, it was during the 1932 World Series against the Chicago Cubs. But ask any fan about that series and he or she will mention the "called shot" that Ruth hit deep into the centerfield bleachers at Wrigley Field in Game 3, not the fact that in the four-game Series, Gehrig batted .529, drove in eight runs, and hit three homers, one of which came on the pitch immediately following Ruth's called shot. But Gehrig harbored no ill-feelings. In his farewell address to 61,808 fans at Yankee Stadium on July 4, 1939, he spoke the now legendary words: "Fans, for the past two weeks you have been reading about a bad break I got. Yet today I consider myself the luckiest man on the face of the earth...." Gehrig died on June 2, 1941, 16 years to the day after he had earned a starting slot on the Yankees roster, and just 17 days shy of his 38th birthday.

generations, between 1923 and '64, the Bronx Bombers never played more than four seasons without winning a World Series. Even a world war couldn't stop them. The Yanks didn't triumph solely at Okinawa and Omaha Beach; they kept on winning in the Bronx, too, capturing the World Series in '41 and '43. Perhaps catcher Yogi Berra best summed up the sentiments of his team's frustrated opponents when he said, "It ain't over 'til it's over."

In the Yankees dugout, greatness begat greatness. Just two seasons after Babe Ruth left the Bronx in 1934, a skinny California kid named Joe DiMaggio arrived as a rookie. Mickey Mantle arrived on the scene in '51, DiMaggio's last season, and assumed DiMaggio's post in centerfield the next year. The team has retired so many numbers that the Yankees may soon have to go into triple-digits. The immortalized numbers are Billy Martin's 1, Ruth's 3, Lou Gehrig's 4, DiMaggio's 5, Mantle's 7, Bill Dickey's and Berra's 8, Roger Maris's 9, Phil Rizzuto's 10, Thurman Munson's 15, Ford's 16, Don Mattingly's 23, Elston Howard's 32, Casey Stengel's 37 and Reggie Jackson's 44. As of 1997, a total of 24 players, managers and executives who spent the defining years of their careers with the Yankees were enshrined in the Hall of Fame in Cooperstown, New York. There are so many pinstripe legends that in 1932 the Yankees decided to build their

18

own monument park inside Yankee Stadium to honor them all.

Naturally, this franchise spawned what most historians regard as the greatest single team in baseball history. The 1927 Yankees, a.k.a. Murderer's Row, won 110 games and lost 44, an American League record that would stand for 27 seasons. In front of a crowd of nearly 75,000 fans on Opening Day at Yankee Stadium, Waite Hoyt defeated the Philadelphia Athletics 8–3 to put the Yankees in first place, where they would remain for the entire season. The team batting average was .307 and the slugging percentage was an alltime record .489. That Yankees club launched 158 home runs, 102 more than any other

DiMaggio's classic swing (opposite page) produced a 56-game hitting streak, one of baseball's seemingly unassailable marks; the crafty Stengel (below, left) managed the Yankees to seven of their 23 World Series titles.

In SI's Words

Stengel has revolutionized baseball since he took over as manager of the Yankees in 1949 by using the players on his bench not as replacements in an emergency but as extra troops to be held in reserve in each game until the proper time comes to commit them. Most of the other clubs in major league baseball have begun to recognize the advantages of this system, but many of them still can't seem to get shed of the old idea that if you have two good third basemen (or whatever) you keep one and trade the other for a pitcher. Stengel hangs on to both....

The result is that Stengel right now has 13 topflight major league infielders and outfielders to juggle in and out around Mantle and Berra. Each feels he is good enough to be a rightful regular, and when he finds himself in the lineup, he plays his skillful, daring, opportunistic heart out to prove his real worth to Stengel. Casey observes the man's abilities and how he utilizes them, makes a few mental notes and several thousand oral ones. Then, when he wants a player who can hit a ground ball to the right side with one out and a man on third base, he knows whether to use, say, Noren or Collins against a pitcher who tends to keep the ball low, say, or high.

—Robert Creamer, July 23, 1956

American League team. Heck, Ruth hit a major league record 60 long balls, outhomering every other ballclub in the league by himself. Ruth also batted .356 with 164 RBI, which should have been good enough for a Triple Crown except that his own teammate, Gehrig, hit .373 with 175 RBI. During batting practice before Game 1 of the World Series at Pittsburgh's Forbes Field, the ferocious Yankee lineup that included Ruth, Gehrig, Bob Meusel, Tony Lazzeri, Earle Combs and Joe Dugan supposedly so intimidated the Pirates that they were eventually swept in four straight games.

Is it any surprise that baseball's two most celebrated individual feats were accomplished by Yankees players? In 1941 DiMaggio got at least one hit in a record 56 straight games, and in 1961 Maris hit 61 homers. But those accomplishments are merely the highlights for a franchise steeped in legend. What about the monumental day in 1925 when first baseman Wally Pipp suffered a headache and was replaced by Gehrig, who went on to play the next 2,130 games before succumbing to a terminal disease that would thereafter bear his name? Or the time Ruth visited a hospital and a dying boy named Johnny Sylvester asked the Sultan of Swat to hit a home run for him? Ruth hit two homers that afternoon and the boy shrugged off his illness. Or Game 3 of the 1932 World Series against the Cubs at

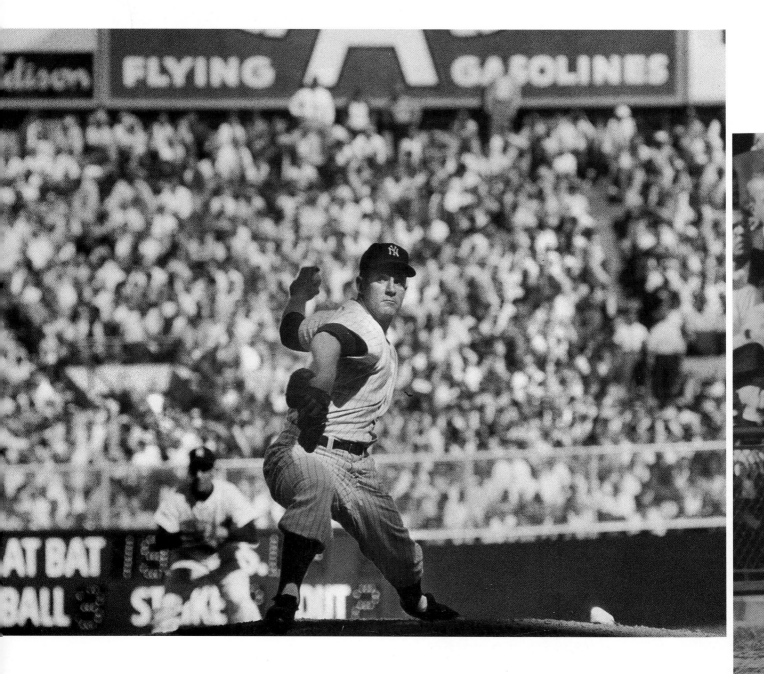

Wrigley Field, when Ruth pointed his bat toward the centerfield bleachers and hit a home run to that spot on the very next pitch? Then there is Mantle's 565-foot home run in 1953 that sailed completely out of Washington D.C.'s Griffith Stadium, the longest home run ever hit. And Don Larsen's perfect game against the Brooklyn Dodgers in the 1956 Fall Classic. There is Jackson, Mr. October, launching three homers on three pitches in Game 6 of the '77 World Series to beat the Los Angeles Dodgers and nail down another Yankees championship. And there is Bucky Dent's home run in a 1978 playoff game at Fenway Park, which transformed the shortstop into Boston's most notorious villain since the Strangler.

Who could have imagined all this from a team with such humble beginnings? The franchise was born in 1903 in a hardscrabble little ballyard in Upper Manhattan called Hilltop Park. Those original Yankees were called the Highlanders, but, alas, they never

21

Ford (far left) spent his entire 16-year career as a Yankee, winning 236 games and a record 10 in the World Series. Berra (above), a legendary coiner of phrases, was also a terrific clutch hitter; Mantle (left) hit 536 home runs, among them some of the longest in baseball history.

found high ground in the American League standings. In 1913 the team's name was changed to the Yankees, but the results remained desultory until Boston owner Harry Frazee sold Ruth to New York in 1920 for $125,000. The Bambino promptly stepped into the spotlight in a town made for superstars. Ruth led the Yankees to their first-ever pennant in 1921. He hit a game-winning homer on Opening Day 1923 in the brand new stadium that would come to be known as The House That Ruth Built. To close out that season the Yankees beat the New York Giants in the first Subway Series. The Yanks would win two more World Series in the '20s, shifting the balance of power to the Bronx. During those halcyon days in the '20s, Yankees owner Jacob Ruppert once outlined his ideal afternoon at Yankee Stadium. "It's when the Yankees score eight runs in the first inning," Ruppert said, "and then slowly pull away."

The Yankees have continued to thrive over the years by adjusting quickly to the game's innovations and rules changes. Early in the century, when it was fashionable to purchase players from poorer teams, the Yankees were always ahead of the market curve. During the ensuing decades, when farm systems ruled the sport, the Bombers cultivated some of baseball's most fertile soil. Finally, when free agency took hold in the '70s, the Yankees doled out the necessary cash to assemble the best talent in baseball.

Jackson (left) loved the Series stage—his three home runs in 1977's Game 6 will forever be a part of Series lore; the latest Yankees triumph, in 1996, was no less joyous for being the team's 23rd (right).

The franchise has also been managed by some of the game's craftiest minds, from Miller Huggins to Joe McCarthy to Stengel. It was Stengel who led the Yankees to 10 pennants in 12 seasons from 1949 to '60, a ruthless reign that gave rise to the famous cry, "Break Up The Yankees!"

Hundreds of years from now sports historians will refer to the twentieth century as the Century of the New York Yankees. The history of the team is basically the history of baseball so far. The Yankees have even transcended sports, becoming part of the fabric of American life. The team and its players have been immortalized in songs such as *Joltin' Joe DiMaggio*. Hollywood has depicted the franchise in films such as *The Pride of the Yankees*. And Broadway twice scored a hit with a play called *Damn Yankees*, a musical about how the Devil broke up the Yankees dynasty.

Exactly how far-reaching is the Yankees mystique? During the 1987 superpower summit in Washington D.C., President Ronald Reagan invited Joe DiMaggio to a state dinner to honor Soviet president Mikhail Gorbachev. Upon being introduced to the Yankee Clipper, both statesmen pulled out baseballs for DiMaggio to sign. DiMaggio was asked what he would cherish most about his remarkable career. "It wasn't the records, the Hall of Fame, none of that," DiMaggio said. "I'm most proud that I was a Yankee."

2

24 Bob Cousy once called it the most arrogant act in the history of sports. With the clock running out on a Boston Celtics victory, Red Auerbach would pull a Hoyo de Monterrey cigar out of his breast pocket, slowly peel off the wrapper, sniff the length of the stogie, ease it into his mouth and light it. At that precise moment, the latest Celtics victims knew they had been smoked. For many years, the final buzzer wasn't necessary at Boston Garden. The game ended when Auerbach torched his Victory Cigar. "I thought it was funny," Bill Russell said. "The cigar was part of what made the Celtics who we were."

Frustrated Celtics opponents called it unsportsmanlike conduct. Auerbach called it Celtic Pride. He grew to revel in how much his unique celebration rankled the enemy, and when the league ordered Auerbach to stop, he shrugged and kept right on smoking. Auerbach concerned himself only with winning. One of his favorite aphorisms was one he swiped from Knute Rockne: "Show me a good loser and I'll show you a loser."

What kind of loser was Auerbach? It was tough to tell through all that cigar smoke. Sixteen times Auerbach triumphantly lit a stogie after the final NBA game of the season. No other team in the league can claim 16 championships. No other team in any sport has come close to winning eight rings in a row. It should also be footnoted that in only three of the Celtics trips to the NBA finals did they not walk away with the trophy. Therein lies the Celtic Mystique. As a result, there are 18 Celtics players enshrined at the Hall of Fame in Springfield, Mass., and 18 players whose numbers have been retired. The franchise's tradition is so dense that new Celtics are dismayed to discover that only jersey number 20 is still available between 14 and 25.

When the Celtics arrived in Boston in 1946, it marked the beginning of a distinct change of mindset in the city, lending credence to Auerbach's theory that "the Celtics are more than a basketball team, they're a way of life." In the '40s basketball programs were not even offered in the

Auerbach (left) and his stogie became an annoying and ubiquitous sight for opponents; before Bird vs.

Magic became the marquee matchup, there was Russell against Wilt Chamberlain (far right).

Boston high schools. Bostonians were totally devoted to baseball and hockey and the Celtics were deemed necessary only to fill the empty winter nights when the Bruins were out of town. Attendance at most Celtics games was less than 4,000 and editors grudgingly gave at most a paragraph to the team in the morning papers. The ballclub nearly folded after its first three unremarkable seasons, but in 1950 Auerbach showed up with enough chutzpah to keep the team afloat. Auerbach would serve as coach, general manager and president over the next four decades, winning championships and cultivating enemies throughout the NBA.

The theme of Auerbach's early seasons as the Celtics coach was generally close, but no cigar. Cousy was the first Celtics luminary, a 6' 1" point guard

with peripheral vision as vast as that of anybody who ever played the game. Engineering the Celtics' fast break, Cousy regularly led the league in assists, and his team led the league in scoring for five straight seasons, but struggled mightily in the postseason. Auerbach envied the intimidating effects of Minneapolis Lakers center George Mikan and realized Boston could never win a title without a force on defense.

Legend has it that Celtics owner Walter Brown convinced the Rochester Royals to pass on Bill Russell with the first pick in the '56 draft by agreeeing to steer the Ice Capades to Rochester for two years. Russell fell to the Celtics and promptly proved he could dominate a game without scoring a single point. Russell rebounded, he threw pinpoint outlet

passes to ignite the Boston break and he turned blocking shots into an art form long before rejections were even counted as an official stat. "Bill put a whole new sound in pro basketball," Auerbach says. "The sound of his footsteps."

The Celtics dynasty was hatched during the '56–'57 season, when Boston reached the NBA finals for the first time and met the St. Louis Hawks. The series lasted seven games and in the deciding game Tom Heinsohn scored 37 points and Russell grabbed 32 rebounds to lead the Celtics to a 125–123 victory in double overtime and the team's first NBA title.

After losing in the championship finals in '58, the Celtics then began a run of unparalleled success. From '59 to '66 the Celtics captured eight straight NBA titles. The opponents fell like ducks in a shooting gallery. Boston beat Minneapolis in four games in '59, St. Louis in seven in '60, the Hawks again in five in '61, the Los Angeles Lakers in seven in '62, the Lakers in six in '63, the San Francisco Warriors in five in '64, the Lakers in five in '65 and the Lakers in seven in '66. "We never got tired of winning," Cousy said. "We'd come back for training camp every year with saliva dripping off our lips, saying 'Kill, kill, kill, I want another title.'"

Auerbach, Russell, Sam Jones and K.C. Jones were the only constants throughout the

Cousy became the first master of the no-look pass (below); Havlicek's steal (left) to seal the Celtics' win over the Sixers in the 1965 conference finals is a cherished Boston highlight.

27

Aftermath

Of our three dynasties, only the Celtics have not checked in with a title in the 1990s to keep their glory updated. The Montreal Canadiens captured the Stanley Cup in '93, and the Yankees triumphed in the World Series in '96. The Celtics last reached the NBA finals in '87, when they lost in six games to the Lakers, and since Larry Bird retired in 1992, the league's most storied franchise has struggled.

Four straight losing seasons were capped in 1996–97 by a franchise-worst record of 15–67—the championship '85–'86 season turned on its head. Celtics management had had enough, and sought relief in the form of energetic young coach Rick Pitino, who had just led the University of Kentucky to two straight NCAA finals. Pitino received an astonishingly lucrative deal, and brought in a slew of young players, among them Kentucky products Ron Mercer and Antoine Walker. The Pitino era began in style, with a 92–85 opening-night victory over the defending champion Chicago Bulls. Though the young team would experience growing pains, few in the Boston area doubted that restored glory was just a few seasons away.

Russell (left) was an acrobat around the boards, leading the league in rebounding four times and averaging an astonishing 22.5 per game for his career; by the time he retired in 1969, he had collected 11 championship rings.

run. Cousy and Heinsohn retired along the way and were replaced by Satch Sanders and John Havlicek. Those Celtics teams were so incessantly good that the trophies actually began to lose their luster. Remembering the time in '65 when Boston reeled off 20 straight points while destroying the Lakers in the title-clinching victory, Russell wrote, "We were not just beating this team. We were destroying it. That was my worst moment in sports. There was the horror of the destruction, not the joy of winning."

Russell took over as player-coach in '67 and Auerbach focused on his duties as general manager, which included a dozen years of semi-struggle after Russell's 1969 retirement before he was able to restore the team to greatness. But rumors of

In SI's Words

There has never been a basketball player quite like the Celtics' Larry Joe Bird, in whom talent and tenacity rage a daily wire-to-wire battle for supremacy. Owing to the extraordinary importance of the giant pivotman in the game, it is probably impossible to declare that, in his seventh season, the 6' 9", 220-pound Bird, a forward, is greater than Bill Russell, Wilt Chamberlain or Kareem Abdul-Jabbar—that is, the greatest player of all time. Or maybe it isn't.

"Before Bird I used to vacillate," says Bob Cousy, now a Celtics broadcaster. "The question didn't seem relevant. But Bird came along with *all* the skills, *all* the things a basketball player has to do. I think he's the greatest...." And there comes this weighty word from Westwood. "I've always considered Oscar Robertson to be the best player in the game," says John Wooden. "Now I'm not so sure that Larry Bird isn't." Even Laker general manager Jerry West, who refuses to compare players from different eras, says of Bird, "He is as nearly perfect as you can get in almost every phase of basketball."

—Jack McCallum, March 3, 1986

Boston's demise were always premature. Even during the Celtics "lean" years they still won more than their share of NBA titles.

In the late '60s, Havlicek emerged as the team's transcendent star, scoring 40 points in the clinching game against the Lakers as Boston won another championship in '68. The Celtics repeated the feat in seven games against Los Angeles in '69. In '71 Dave Cowens joined Havlicek and Jo Jo White to form the hub of a new generation. This group brought another title to Boston in '74 and yet another in '76. After 16 seasons, Havlicek retired in '78, the same year that Auerbach drafted a junior from Indi-

ana State who wouldn't even join the Celtics until after he played his senior season.

While awaiting the arrival of Larry Bird, the Celtics bottomed out in '79, finishing with an abysmal 29–53 record. In Bird's rookie season the Celtics won 61 games. After adding Kevin McHale and Robert Parish through a trade with Golden State in '80, Boston won the '81 NBA title over Houston in six games. After losing in the playoffs in '82 and '83 under the iron fist of coach Bill Fitch, Auerbach tinkered once again. He traded for defensive guard Dennis Johnson and then hired mild-mannered K.C. Jones as the new coach.

After McHale (below) joined the Celtics in 1980, they won their first championship in five years; the nucleus of McHale, Bird and Parish would go on to win two more in the '80s.

30

Jones basically gave Bird the wheel, and the Celtics won the '84 title by beating the Lakers in seven games in one of a series of epic clashes between Bird and Magic Johnson.

In '86 the Celtics brandished their most talented lineup ever. They won 67 games in the regular season and shot better than 50% as a team while leading the league in rebounding. Bird collected a pair of triple-doubles in the NBA finals as Boston again defeated Houston. Naturally, in the closing moments of that series, Auerbach pulled out his stogie and the Rockets suffered the humiliation of the Victory Cigar, as so many teams before them had done.

When Bird (below, right) arrived in the 1979–80 season, he began a new era in Boston; his uncanny shooting touch and sheer competitiveness simply made his teammates better.

"I always dreamed of coming back to beat the Celtics," Lakers Hall of Famer Elgin Baylor once said, "and taking the cigar out of Red's mouth and puffing on it just once."

It was a common fantasy around the league, carried to extremes by the Cincinnati Royals. One day the Celtics played a game in Cincinnati and 5,000 cigars were passed out to the arriving fans. The spectators planned to fire up their stogies in the final moments of Cincinnati's victory over the Celtics. Alas, only one cigar was lit that day, and it belonged to Auerbach. The foul smoke wafted through the Cincinnati Gardens. It smelled like victory.

31

Montreal Canadiens

3

How many? It's the most hackneyed question in sports. Except in Montreal, where they stopped counting ages ago. Canadiens fans have always been more intrigued by another question. *How?* In spite of all the Stanley Cups the Montreal Canadiens have won over eight decades of brilliant hockey, the Canadiens dynasty will always be celebrated more for its magnificent style.

The franchise is the very embodiment of Gallic flair. It is hockey's representation of a distinctly French appreciation of elegance and speed with a little conceit thrown in for good measure. To think of the Canadiens is to think of much more than the myriad banners that hang from the Montreal Forum's rafters. They are the "Flying Frenchmen," their glorious manes wafting in the breeze as they glide swiftly through center ice. Yes, it's the hair that connects them, from the bushy black locks of Jack Laviolette in the 1918 to the golden strands of Guy Lafleur in the 1978.

The Canadiens built their empire in their fortress, and the soldiers dressed in a classic sweater, *La Seinte Flanelle*—the sacred flannel. Across their chests they wore the most regal crest in sports, CH, which stood for the *Club de Hockey Canadien.*

If you insist on counting, the Canadiens won 24 Stanley Cups from 1916 through 1993, more championships than any other franchise in baseball, basketball, football or hockey. Montreal has sent 39 players to the Hall of Fame, by far the most of any team. Ten Canadiens coaches are also enshrined there. At its zenith in the late '50s, Montreal won five straight Stanley Cups, and in the late '70s the club reached the mountaintop again, this time stringing together four titles. History suggests that the Canadiens arrive in intermittent yet devastating waves.

Dryden (left), Savard (center) and Robinson made the Canadiens of the '70s one of the strongest defensive teams in NHL history.

34

The proud Canadiens were born of Montreal's French-speaking citizens and their desire to be a part of big league sports. To ensure the continued association between the team's players and the community, in 1909 the National Hockey Association granted the newly-formed Canadiens the right to sign only French-speaking players. Hence the Canadiens' other nickname, *Les Habitants de Montréal*, or Habs, for short. Although the rule was softened several years later, French-speaking players from the province of Quebec have always predominated on Canadiens teams. The Habs were a great source of pride to Montreal's French community, and the team came to be so highly esteemed that many of its players, most notably Maurice Richard, were intentionally overlooked by the Canadian army during World War II because it was thought that they would contribute more to the war effort by boosting morale at home.

The Canadiens can be divided into eras of brilliance, each defined by a few luminous players. The pioneer of Montreal's initial period of Stanley Cup

Richard (above), the first player to score 50 goals in an NHL season, may have been the most beloved Canadien of all; Plante (right), who later became the first goalie to wear a mask, was just one in a long line of Vezina winners in Montreal.

success, in the early '30s, was Aurel Joliat, a tiny wing who wore a black baseball cap and dared opponents to knock it off his head. Joliat was eventually joined by center Howie Morenz, dubbed the Stratford Streak, who was considered the Babe Ruth of hockey. Morenz was renowned for his blistering speed and his headlong rushes on goal. Soon the Forum came to be known as the House that Morenz Built. Joliat and Morenz led the Canadiens to back-to-back Stanley Cups in '30 and '31.

Morenz died of a heart attack at the age of 34 in 1937, and his funeral was held at center ice in the Forum. The heartsick Canadiens plunged into a period of despair. The club's popularity dipped so low during the late '30s that the owners considered turning the Forum into a streetcar garage and folding the team, or moving the franchise to, of all places, Cleveland.

Five dark years passed before the arrival of Maurice (Rocket) Richard, who sparked memories of Morenz with his recklessness and fury on the ice. Richard returned the Canadiens to their lofty perch

in 1944, leading the squad to the Stanley Cup following a regular season in which Montreal lost only five games. Richard set a playoff record with 12 goals in nine games, including five in one semifinal contest against the Toronto Maple Leafs.

The following season Richard scored 50 goals in 50 games as the anchor of Montreal's devastating Punch Line, which also featured Toe Blake and Elmer Lach. Richard, a product of the backstreets of Montreal, rapidly became the most popular Canadien of his era, galvanizing the Forum whenever he barreled across the ice. On frozen ponds across Quebec children wore his number 9, taped

their sticks like his and even dabbed grease in their hair to mimic the Rocket. Some of those kids eventually became his teammates. Among them were Bernard (Boom Boom) Geoffrion, the team clown, who married Morenz's daughter and pioneered the modern slapshot; Jean Beliveau, a fluid skater with a deft scoring touch; and Maurice's kid brother, Henri, (the Pocket Rocket), who became a member of Maurice's line.

The true testament to the Rocket's enormous popularity occurred in 1955, when he was suspended from the final three regular season games and the playoffs by NHL president Clarence Campbell for

engaging in some unruly behavior with a linesman. When Campbell showed up for a game at the Forum soon after, he was bombarded with rotten vegetables and a melee ensued that forced the game to be canceled. The incident became known as the Richard Riot.

Montreal would win eight Stanley Cups during the Rocket's 17 years in a Canadiens jersey. He retired in 1960 with 544 regular season goals and 82 more in the playoffs. Beliveau took the reins as captain in 1961 and led Montreal to titles in '65, '66, '68, '69 and '71. Then, with Henri Richard as captain, Montreal won another Cup in '73.

In the mid-'70s the Canadiens entered their last era of sustained greatness. From 1976 to '79 the team won four straight Stanley Cups and put together a record of 229-46-45. In 1977 they set an alltime NHL record by suffering no defeats in 38 straight home games. They were the most balanced Canadiens team ever, combining the offensive firepower of Guy Lafleur, Jacques Lemaire and Yvan Cournoyer with the finest defensive trio in hockey—Larry Robinson, Serge Savard and Guy Lapointe.

Those late '70s Cup winners also featured rangy goaltender Ken Dryden, who in eight seasons with the Canadiens won 80 of 112 playoff games and six Stanley Cups. Dryden was a part of Montreal's line of superb goalies that traces all the way back to the '20s and Georges Vezina. Two years after the legendary Vezina left the game in '25, the first Vezina trophy was awarded to the league's top goalie, Montreal's George Hainsworth. Through 1997 the trophy

37

Three of the smoothest skaters to grace the Forum were Lafleur (left), Beliveau (above, middle) and Cournoyer (above, left), all continuing the tradition of French-speaking Canadiens stars.

The Mountaintop

If you're a Montreal Canadiens fan, your loyalty is rewarded with a Stanley Cup title, oh, every five years or so. You can count on it. Check the record. Other franchises may generate a head of steam, but it seems Montreal always interrupts them to reestablish itself as the NHL's top dog. The mountaintop? The Canadiens have a base camp at the summit, and can walk out almost anytime to enjoy the view. They won their first Stanley Cup in 1916, and made the NHL finals in 1918 and '19, the first two years of the league's existence. They won the Stanley Cup in '24, and again in '30. A repeat Cup in '31 gave way to the longest title drought in franchise history, 13 whole years.

In the 1950s Montreal built that luxury suite on top of the mountain. That decade they went to the Stanley Cup finals *every year*, and won six titles. The Habs briefly gave way to Toronto in the early '60s, as the Maple Leafs won three in a row. But back came the Canadiens in 1965 to interrupt them. Montreal closed the '60s with back-to-back Cups and owned the '70s outright, winning six titles, including four straight to round out the bellbottom era. When Edmonton began to dominate in the mid '80s, their four-title run was sandwiched around a Montreal title, in '86. After Pittsburgh won two Cups in '91 and '92, in swooped the Canadiens in '93 to win their 24rd championship, a record for professional sports.

went to a Canadien 26 more times. Bill Durnan, who once had four consecutive shutouts, won the Vezina six times in the '40s. Jacques Plante, who won six Stanley Cups from '53 to '60 and was the first goalie to wear a facemask, captured six Vezinas. Dryden won the trophy five times. More recently Patrick Roy won three Vezina trophies and the 1993 Stanley Cup as a Canadien.

Many current Canadiens admit they are awed and overwhelmed by the team's tradition and history of success. For years an intimidating challenge has been painted above the lockers in the Montreal dressing room. TO YOU FROM FAILING HANDS WE THROW THE TORCH. BE YOURS TO HOLD IT HIGH.

And indeed the torch has been passed across decades from artists to apprentices, from Laviolette to Joliat to Morenz to Richard to Beliveau to Lafleur, the spell never broken. Through the years the Canadiens have been a team so graceful, so lyric, that they inspired poets. Summing up the Habs in one line of verse, Quebecois author Felix Leclerc once wrote, "It's the wind skating."

Dryden (left), astonishingly agile at 6' 4" and 210 pounds, may have been the toughest goalie to beat in NHL history; Scotty Bowman (above) presided over five of Montreal's Stanley Cup titles; Denis Savard (right) was a member of the last Cup winner in 1993.

What makes Toronto tick?" asked the TV announcer. "What makes Toronto dead?" Maurice (The Rocket) Richard asked back. Richard, who has played right wing for the Club de Hockey Canadien, Inc. every winter since 1942, sat, his shoes off, in a dark room in the Royal York hotel, laughing at Red Skelton and smoking a cigar ... Next week, as their captain, [Richard] leads the Canadiens toward their fifth consecutive Stanley Cup. "It's getting to be my time now," he had said in the men's room of a Montreal–Detroit sleeper several days before. "I'm getting near the end. I have had some good times, some bad. I started out with three bad injuries [fractured left ankle, left wrist, right ankle] and am ending with three bad injuries [sliced Achilles' tendon, fractured left tibia, depressed fracture of facial bone]. The old days are gone. These are the new days. I'll never score five goals in one night." He looked out the window at the dismal, glaring snow, listening to the wheels as the train bore him to his 1,091st game. Behind him, the glorious past, the records: 50 goals (and in a 50-game season); five goals in a playoff game; 18 winning goals in 14 playoff series, six of which were in overtime....

—Gilbert Rogin, March 21, 1960

Teams of a Decade

Uneasy rests the head that wears the crown. Yeah, right. Whoever uttered those words obviously was not a fan of any of the teams in this chapter. These teams didn't settle for just one crown. All of them repeated. Many of them repeated repeatedly. By collecting a handful of rings in a relatively brief period of time, each team here has earned the next best label to that of dynasty. Each is a *Team of a Decade*.

Not only did all of these clubs clearly dominate their respective sports over a ten-year period, but they also behaved in strict accordance with the calendar. Each team selected a specific decade; the '50s, '70s, '90s or whatever, and stamped it as its own. For football fans, the Pittsburgh Steelers of Franco Harris and Terry Bradshaw and the Steel Curtain defense defined the '70s. Magic Johnson's Los Angeles Lakers, who won five NBA championships with their Showtime offense are clearly that league's Team of the '80s. Coach Vince Lombardi's rugged Green Bay Packers, who won five NFL titles and two Super Bowls, are icons of the '60s. Wayne Gretzky and the Edmonton Oilers captured four Stanley Cups in

The mighty Packers, endowed with a ferocious defense (left), were without a doubt the NFL's Team of the '60s.

the '80s, and the team added a fifth in '90 after the Great One had departed for Los Angeles. A similar story unfolded with George Mikan and the Minneapolis Lakers in the '50s. Michael Jordan carried the Chicago Bulls to a three-peat plus two more in the '90s. Joe Montana and the San Francisco 49ers outfoxed the rest of the NFL in the '80's. And finally, those old enough can recall how the powerful Maple Leafs provided some welcome joy around Toronto in the post–World War II '40s.

I suspect that the Cleveland Browns' No. 11

ranking will be the most controversial in this chapter, and perhaps the entire book. The gritty Browns of Otto Graham and Marion Motley did reach a championship game in 10 consecutive seasons and won an incredible seven titles, but it's important to remember that the first four of those titles occurred in the All-America Football Conference, a clearly inferior league. I also expect that seeding the Cincinnati Reds No. 7 will

raise some eyebrows. I understand that the Reds won only two World Series, but The Big Red Machine of Johnny Bench, Joe Morgan, Tony Perez and Pete Rose was nothing short of a phenomenon in the '70s, and the '76 edition of the Reds was the best team ever to play in the National League.

It's safe to say that none of these teams left anything to prove. Their heads rested easy despite all the crowns.

The Browns (clockwise from upper left) of Edgar Jones, Graham, Motley and Lou Saban) were great, but in an inferior league; Abdul-Jabbar (below, left) and the Lakers dominated the '80s; Bench (below) and the Reds were '70s superstars.

45

The Steel Curtain, led by Greene (75) and Lambert (58), held its opponents to just 28 points in the last nine games of the 1976 season.

Pittsburgh's Immaculate Conception began with the Immaculate Reception. In a 1972 AFC playoff game at Three Rivers Stadium, the Steelers trailed the Oakland Raiders 7–6 with 22 seconds left in the game and faced a fourth down on their 40-yard line when Terry Bradshaw threw a desperation pass over the middle to Frenchy Fuqua. The ball was deflected by Raiders safety Jack Tatum and caught just before it hit the Astroturf by Pittsburgh rookie Franco Harris, who sprinted 42 yards into the end zone for the most improbable game-winning touchdown in NFL history. "Up until that point I was the only one who believed that this was a good football team," Steelers coach Chuck Noll said. "That play was a sign that this was a team of destiny."

It is a gross understatement to say that the Steelers were due. That game represented the first postseason victory in Pittsburgh's first 40 football seasons, a period during which the team had earned the dubious distinction of laughingstock of the league. The franchise had recorded only eight winning seasons over its miserable history and had perpetrated some of the NFL's worst personnel decisions, such as cutting a young quarterback named Johnny Unitas one day in 1955. So nobody was shocked when Penn State's Joe Paterno turned down the Steelers coaching job before the 1969 season and the post fell to an obscure line coach from the Baltimore Colts named Noll. In his first speech to his team he announced that his goal was to win the Super Bowl, which produced some muffled snickers around the locker room. Sure enough, that team won its opener against the Detroit Lions, and then lost 13 games in a row.

Noll's plan was to build gradually through the draft. He selected defensive linemen Joe Greene and L.C.

Beloved Steelers owner Art Rooney had to wait 42 years for his first NFL championship; Swann (right) and his acrobatic catches, including a pair of gems in Super Bowl X, remain a staple of highlight films.

48

Greenwood in '69 and then won a coin flip in '70 for the right to pick Bradshaw. Noll preached teamwork, epitomized in a message he once posted on the bulletin board in the Steelers' dressing room: WHEN GEESE FLY IN FORMATION, THEY TRAVEL 70% FASTER THAN WHEN THEY FLY ALONE.

After winning the dramatic playoff opener in 1972, the Steelers lost their next game to the Miami Dolphins, who were steamrolling their way to an undefeated season. In '73 Oakland earned its revenge by knocking Pittsburgh out of the playoffs in a 33–14 rout.

Then in '74 the Steelers won the AFC Central Division as Bradshaw developed a synergy with his rookie wide receivers, Lynn Swann and John Stallworth. Pittsburgh's defense took over in the playoffs and muzzled Minnesota 16–6 in Super Bowl IX to capture the Steelers' first NFL title in their 42-year history. Pittsburgh won a second straight championship by defeating Dallas 21–17 in Super Bowl X.

The team's trademark was its Steel Curtain defense, which truly deserved the nickname in '76. Led by Greene, Greenwood, linebackers Jack Ham and Jack Lambert and cornerback Mel Blount, the defense ensured the Steelers nine straight victories at the end of that season. During those nine wins, five opponents were shut out and Pittsburgh yielded just one touchdown and a total of only 28 points. Unfortunately, Harris and fellow running back Rocky Bleier were both injured in an opening-round playoff win and the Steelers were then eliminated by Oakland. After winning another Central Division title in '77, the Steelers lost to the Denver Broncos in the opening round of the playoffs.

In 1978 Noll overhauled the Steelers, shifting the

In SI's Words

As the closest thing to combat in civilian life, professional football is a breeding ground of legends that echo our rapidly fading warrior past. Reputedly the fiercest of these nascent legendary figures is Jack Lambert, the All-Pro middle linebacker of the Pittsburgh Steelers who after only two years in the NFL wears two Super Bowl rings on his fingers.

"Jack Lambert is so mean," says Pittsburgh Tackle Mean Joe Greene, a legend in his own right, "that he don't even like *himself.*"

Ever since Sam Huff of the New York Giants first popularized the sadomasochistic side of the middle linebacker's role in the early 1960s, pro football has seen a steady stream of larger-than-death monsters parading through the position, each one trying to be meaner, fiercer more bloodthirstily outrageous than the next....

The latest ogre is John Harold Lambert, better known as "Smilin' Jack" because of his dour visage, who at age 24 has risen to the top of the demonological heap more rapidly than any other legend in a sport that thrives on them. And he doesn't like the legend one bit. This is precisely how mean Jack Lambert can be.

—Robert F. Jones, July 12, 1976

offense into a more pass-oriented scheme. That team finished the regular season with a 14–2 record and is considered by many to be the best in NFL history. Bradshaw passed for a record four touchdowns and 318 yards in a 35–31 win over Dallas in Super Bowl XIII as Pittsburgh became the first team to win three Super Bowls. The following season Bradshaw nailed down a 31–19 victory over the Los Angeles Rams in Super Bowl XIV with another aerial show that included a decisive 73-yard go-ahead touchdown to Stallworth with just under three minutes remaining.

From 1972 to '79, Pittsburgh pieced together a record-tying streak of eight seasons in the playoffs,

including six consecutive AFC titles, and Noll became the only NFL coach ever to win four Super Bowls. A total of 22 Steelers played in all four Super Bowl victories, and seven of them—Greene, Bradshaw, Harris, Ham, Lambert, Blount and center Mike Webster—are in the Hall of Fame. But age eventually caught up with those Steelers. More precisely, they all grew old at once.

Although the team never captured the elusive fifth ring, the "one for the thumb," Noll's geese proved the power of flying in formation. "We got the wheels in motion and made winning a perpetual thing," Greene said. "We learned that the more you win, the harder it is to lose."

Aftermath

A combination of advancing age and injuries brought the Steelers dynasty to an abrupt close in 1980, a season in which the team went 9–7 and missed the playoffs. Pittsburgh would rise again in '83, as Terry Bradshaw overcame an injured elbow to lead the Steelers to a 10–6 record and a division title. But waiting in the first round of the playoffs were the eventual Super Bowl champion L.A. Raiders, who prevailed 38–10. Bradshaw retired after that season and was inducted into the Hall of Fame in 1989.

With Mark Malone calling signals, the Steelers won their division in '84—despite a 9–7 record—and made it to the AFC title game, where they lost to the Miami Dolphins, 45–28. The lean years that ensued led to coach Chuck Noll's retirement in 1991, after 22 years with the club. Bill Cowher, a native of the Steel City, took over and with Neil O'Donnell at quarterback, Pittsburgh returned to the Super Bowl after the '95 season. O'Donnell threw three interceptions in a 27–17 loss to the Dallas Cowboys.

Harris (left) started the Steelers ascent to greatness with his Immaculate Reception in 1972, and he went on to rush for 1,000 yards or more six times in the next seven seasons; in the last two of Pittsburgh's four championship years, the offense became more pass-oriented, bringing the abilities of Bradshaw (right) to the fore; in Super Bowl XIII, he threw for 318 yards and four touchdowns.

A survey recently conducted by *The Associated Press* asked inner-city kids whom they most admire. Michael Jordan tied for the lead. With God.

For better or worse, that is the lofty circle in which Jordan travels these days. Jordan is no longer a mere basketball player. He has become a messiah with 3% body fat and his name on his shoes. He has spawned a generation of kids who want to be like Mike. Not just American kids. Norweigan kids. Israeli kids. Bolivian kids. In 1992 PBS interviewed a Chinese teenager, asking the boy to list his heros. The young man named two. Revolutionary leader Zhou Enlai and Bulls guard Michael Jordan.

That kind of Q-rating ain't bad for a guy who was cut from his high school basketball team as a sophomore. Since that inauspicious event took place, Jordan has won nine NBA scoring titles and four league MVP awards, all of which means virtually nothing to him. In the process he has also won five NBA championships in the 1990s, which means basically everything.

Since Jordan turned pro in 1985, championships have been the only goals he has struggled to attain. In his rookie year he scored 37 points in his third game. He led the Bulls that season in scoring, rebounding, assists and steals, one of Jordan's many feats that have no precedent in NBA history. For four seasons between '87 and '90, Jordan won the NBA scoring title, but league history shows that players with that distinction rarely win a title. Jordan needed to learn a difficult lesson: that he could not go it alone. The budding superstar wouldn't win a championship until his seventh season, when Bulls coach and Zen mystic Phil Jackson's Triangle offense took hold, giving the other Bulls, dubbed the Jordanaires, something to do other than spectate.

Soon after his arrival in Chicago, Rodman (under basket) became almost as critical to the team as Jordan (top).

53

Part of what makes Chicago's championship era unique is that despite the team's wild success during the '90s, the Bulls roster—other than Jordan and fellow Dream Teamer Scottie Pippen—has been remarkably anonymous. But with each title Jordan came to appreciate his supporting cast more and more. Especially because the Jordanaires developed a penchant for heroism in the NBA Finals. In '91 John Paxson made five critical jump shots in Game 5 to eliminate the Los Angeles Lakers. The following season bench jockeys Scott Williams, Bobby Hansen and Stacey King sparked a rally in Game 6 that polished off Portland. In '93, Paxson sank a clutch three-pointer in Game 6 against Phoenix with just 3.9 seconds left, and Horace Grant blocked the Suns' final rebuttal at the buzzer.

By the time the Bulls won an NBA-record 72 games during the '95–'96 season and captured yet another NBA title, the contributions of Pippen and Dennis Rodman had become nearly as critical as those of Jordan. And it was Steve Kerr who hit the series-clinching jumper in '97 after receiving a pass from Jordan, who was being hounded by most of the Utah team.

Jordan may be best known for aerial acrobatics that lead to thunderous dunks such as the one at right, but he is also among the NBA's finest defenders, as he showed against Clyde Drexler (above) in the 1992 NBA Finals.

Still, while the members of Jordan's supporting cast outdid themselves repeatedly, there was one constant in the Bulls' equation: When Jordan was in a Chicago uniform for an entire season, the Bulls won the title; when he wasn't, they didn't. Which means that Chicago would likely have won seven straight NBA championships had Jordan not retired temporarily to pursue his baseball dream. Without Jordan in '93–'94 and most of '94–'95, the Bulls came up conspicuously short in the playoffs.

Jordan's baseball sojourn illustrated the most refreshing aspect of his personality. He loved to compete and he had absolutely no fear of failure. In fact, one of his countless television commercials reminded us that he had *missed* a potential game-winning shot 26 times in his career. And despite all the basketball minutes that Jordan logged in Chicago, his contracts with the Bulls included an unprecedented "love of the game" clause which allowed him to play hoops anytime he pleased in the offseason. Jordan never considered basketball to be merely a job.

The ledger shows that between '91 and '97, Chicago won five championships in Jordan's five full seasons and the Bulls became the first team to capture three straight titles since the Boston Celtics did

The Mountaintop

Michael Jordan's career has been so brilliant that parts of it get lost in the glare. Consider the fact that he played seven seasons before winning his first championship. *Seven.* **Jordan has been at the summit so long we sometimes forget the climb he made to get there, including three straight bitter playoff losses to the Detroit Pistons, character-building trials by fire that helped forge Chicago's championship mentality. When the Bulls finally broke through in 1991, Jordan, as expected, was the catalyst. In Game 3 of the Eastern Conference finals, His Airness, as the lone defender back, stopped a late-game Detroit fast break and scored 14 points in the fourth quarter to lead Chicago to a 113–107 win that left the Bad Boy Pistons, NBA champions in the previous two seasons, in a bad way, down 3–zip. Then, in Game 4, Jordan scored 29 points and the Bulls swept away their erstwhile nemeses, 115–94, to put the previous three seasons behind them for good and Chicago in the NBA Finals for the first time ever. The Finals themselves were almost anticlimactic, as the Bulls rolled over Magic Johnson and Los Angeles, 4–1. The Lakers, the team of the '80s, were over as the decade they had dominated. The '90s had arrived. So had the Bulls.**

Jackson's Zen approach enabled him (above) to handle his team's competing egos, keeping both Jordan and sec- ond-banana Pippen (right) productive, and yielding a string of NBA titles, includ- ing the Bulls' third in 1993 (far right).

so in 1966. During those seven seasons, the Bulls never lost an NBA Final and were never even pushed to a seventh game. The team averaged more than 60 wins per season and became the only squad ever to win more than 65 regular-season games in three different years. "What we're seeing is something that will never happen again," said Houston Rockets coach Rudy Tomjanovich, whose team gratefully snatched two NBA titles during Jordan's baseball hiatus. "Jordan is the greatest athlete ever. We should all enjoy this while we can."

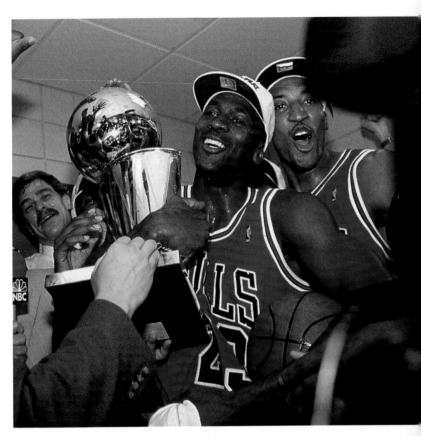

Spotlight

After the Bulls defeated Utah in 1997 to win their fifth NBA title, Michael Jordan, cradling his fifth Finals MVP trophy, pointed to Scottie Pippen and repeated several times, "You're *my* MVP."

It was a telling moment. For while they haven't yet built a monument to Pippen outside the United Center, he is nearly as valuable to the Bulls as Sir Michael is, and Jordan knows it. Pippen's occasional lack of professionalism aside—he once refused to re-enter a playoff game because Phil Jackson had not selected him to take the final shot—he is among the most dangerous and versatile players in the league. His abilities are truly prodigious: He handles the ball like a point guard, plays tenacious man-to-man defense, skywalks as adroitly as the most talented frequent fliers in the league and still can step outside and nail the rainbow three-pointer. Multiple threat indeed.

When Jordan embarked on his excellent baseball adventure in '94–'95, Pippen led the Bulls in scoring, rebounding, assists and steals. And while Pippen sat out the beginning of the '97–'98 season with a foot injury, the Bulls became exactly what they were while Jordan was chasing curves: an NBA also-ran.

6

58

Moments after Vince Lombardi concluded his very first speech as coach of the Green Bay Packers in 1959, quarterback Bart Starr rushed to a nearby pay phone and called his wife, Cherry. "Honey," Starr told her, "we're going to start winning again."

It was a bold statement, considering that the Packers were coming off a horrible '58 season in which Green Bay had a 1-10-1 record and a swiss cheese defense that allowed 32 points per game, the worst in franchise history. NFL officials were so concerned about the negative direction of the Packers, who had endured 11 consecutive years without a winning season, that they were actually contemplating dropping the franchise.

Lombardi wasn't exactly an obvious choice to bring the Pack back. At the time of his hiring he was a 45-year-old assistant coach with the New York Giants who had no head coaching experience at any level above high school. He arrived in Wisconsin with nothing more than his innate ability to command and a portfolio of motivational maxims that would one day be called the Lombardi Credo. The new Green Bay coach loudly lectured his players on commitment to discipline, sacrifice and the relentless struggle to perform at the peak of one's ability. "Talent is not only a blessing," Lombardi often said, "it is also a burden as the great ones find out."

It's tempting to credit the Green Bay players for the team's miraculous turnaround, but the truth is that the Packers roster was not overly talented and it remained relatively constant. As Green Bay began the '59 season, 14 of the 22 starters returned from the forgettable previous season. Lombardi didn't get new players. He made new players out of the ones he had. Lombardi knew he had a decent foundation in Starr, running backs Jim Taylor and Paul Hornung,

When Starr (far right, in helmet) heard his first speech from Lombardi (left), he knew better days were ahead for the Packers.

wide receiver Max McGee, tackle Forrest Gregg and linebacker Ray Nitschke. The group just needed to be "pushed" a little. "He treated us all the same," said defensive tackle Henry Jordan, "like dogs."

Who could have known that Lombardi would soon push his team to five league titles as well as the first two Super Bowl championships in a span of just seven years? Who knew Lombardi was about to transform tiny Green Bay into Titletown, U.S.A.?

There was a foreshadowing of good tidings to come in Lombardi's debut season as the Packers upset coach George Halas's Chicago Bears 9–6 in the opener and went on to finish 7–5 in '59, Green Bay's first winning season in a dozen years. After earning a conference title with an 8–4 record in '60, the Packers lost 17–13 to the Philadelphia Eagles in the NFL championship game, the last title game Lombardi would ever lose as the Green Bay coach.

The Packers captured their first NFL championship in 1961 by beating the New York Giants 37–0 as Hornung tied an NFL postseason record by scoring 19 points in the contest. Green Bay defeated the Giants again, 16–7, to win the NFL title in '62 as Nitschke recovered two fumbles and the underrated defense carried the team. They won another title in '65, defeating the Cleveland Browns 23–12 as Hornung and Taylor combined for more than 200 rushing yards. In 1966 Green Bay defeated the Dallas Cowboys 34–27 to win yet another NFL championship and then moved on to Super Bowl I, where they manhandled the AFL champion Kansas City Chiefs, 35–10.

But the defining game of Lombardi's tenure in Green Bay was yet to come. The 1967 NFL title game against Dallas was a contest better known as the Ice Bowl because it was played on the frozen tundra of Green Bay's Lambeau Field in temperatures hovering around 13 degrees below zero. In a true battle of wills, Lombardi's resolute Packers prevailed when Starr wriggled into the end zone on a quarterback sneak with just 13 seconds left for a 21–17 victory. A routine 33–14 victory over the Oakland Raiders in Super Bowl II gave the Packers their second straight world championship.

Lombardi abandoned his coaching duties following the victory in Super Bowl II because he was mentally exhausted. He had worn himself out driving his aging Packers to the '67 title, regularly hammering the theme that they could be the only team ever to win three straight NFL titles. So far he's right.

A fearsome presence at middle linebacker, Nitschke was the figurative and literal heart of the Packers defense.

60

The kingpin of the Packers' notoriously tough defense, middle linebacker Ray Nitschke struck fear in opponents' hearts. As Nitschke once said, "Linebackers, by the nature of their position, have to be aggressive. If you really love football, that's where you want to be."

If Nitschke's level of aggression was any measure of his love for the game, the bruising tackler from Illinois surely loved football as much as anyone who has ever played, for all 15 years of his pro career. When he entered the league in 1958, he was a 6' 3", 235-pound mass of seething anger and brute strength whose wild ranting and ferocious tackling frightened even his own teammates. Helped by Vince Lombardi's faith and motivated by his "tough love," Nitschke harnessed his aggression successfully enough to earn spots on three All-Pro teams and the MVP award in Green Bay's 1962 NFL Championship victory (16–7) over the New York Giants. "He helped me to turn around as a person," Nitschke said of Lombardi. "He inspired me by his determination." In a classic example of a player's taking on the attributes of his coach, Nitschke seemed at times to control games through pure force of will.

In nine seasons as Green Bay's coach, Lombardi had an 89-29-4 regular-season record, a 9–1 mark in postseason play and his five precious titles. One had to go back 15 years before Lombardi arrived to find another NFL championship in Green Bay, and there wouldn't be another for 29 years after he left. When Lombardi died of cancer in 1970 he became a coaching icon. Future NFL teams would compare themselves to a standard of excellence set by his Packers. They would play for the right to raise the Lombardi Trophy. His legend is almost mythical.

There is a classic tale often told around Titletown that Lombardi arrived home late one night after practice and climbed into bed beside his wife, Marie. "God your feet are cold," Marie said to her husband.

Lombardi responded, "Marie, you can call me Vincent when we're alone."

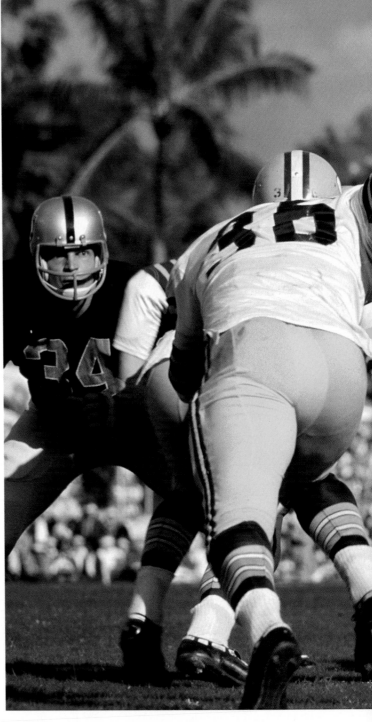

The glamorous Hornung (left) blossomed into a full-blown star after Lombardi's arrival; Starr (above) and the Packers appeared out of place beneath Miami's swaying palm trees, but that hardly prevented them from easily defeating the Raiders, 33–14, in Super Bowl II.

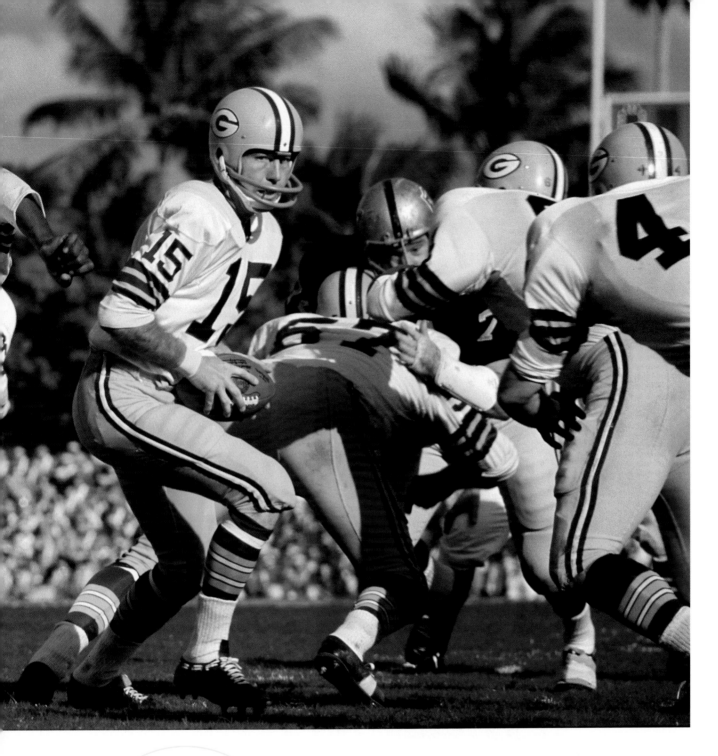

Spotlight

When Vince Lombardi arrived in Green Bay in 1959, he told Paul Hornung to give up his part-time quarterbacking and become a full-time halfback. Overnight, it seemed, Hornung went from first-round draft pick disappointment to superstar, inspiring team leader and consummate playboy. He had sure hands, passed beautifully on the halfback option and was a tenacious and creative runner, a highly effective blocker and an accurate long-distance field goal kicker. In '59, Green Bay's Golden Boy led the league in scoring. In '60, he set an NFL scoring record with 176 points (it still stands), was named league MVP and helped the Packers win the West. Despite commuting from military service in Fort Riley, Kansas, during the '61 season, Hornung again led the NFL in scoring (146 points) and, while on Christmas leave, racked up a record 19 points in Green Bay's 37–0 trouncing of the New York Giants for the team's first title in 17 years. Hornung was handed a one-year suspension for gambling in '63 and after a shaky reentry in '64, was back in rare form by '65, when he scored five touchdowns in a game against the Baltimore Colts. When he retired in '66 after nine seasons, he had 760 career points—62 touchdowns, 190 conversions and 66 field goals.

7

Cincinnati Reds

Bench (left), probably baseball's greatest catcher ever, and Morgan, a rare combination of power and speed, were two vital cogs in the Machine.

Fiery competitor that he was, Rose (right) handled the move from the outfield to third base well, thereby making room for Foster's explosive bat in the lineup.

More than a few people have claimed that the classic nickname was their creation, and Pete Rose is no exception. As Rose recalls, in the late '60s he owned a sporty 1934 Ford, which he dubbed the Little Red Machine, thus inspiring him to refer to his turbocharged Cincinnati ballclub as the Big Red Machine. The phrase first appeared in print on Aug. 4, 1969, the morning after Cincinnati's robust offense beat the Philadelphia Phillies, 19–17, at Philadelphia's Connie Mack Stadium. Before long, The Big Red Machine had become so recognizable that it was

abbreviated to BRM in Ohio newspaper headlines. Reds second baseman Joe Morgan wore a T-shirt featuring the slogan under his jersey for several seasons and the team even requested, and was eventually granted, a copyright on the name. By the time the Reds reached their peak efficiency in the mid-70's, one might have thought their 25 players actually were a humming, ferocious hunk of metal.

Like any machine, the BRM required a human element, and general manager Bob Howsam was the builder of this baseball prototype. In 1970 manager

Foster (left) became an RBI machine in the cleanup spot, driving in 121 runs in '76 and 149 in '77 with his trademark black bat; Bench (above) was a marvel behind the plate, winning the Gold Glove as a rookie and making the honor his personal possession by keeping it for the next nine seasons.

Sparky Anderson arrived to turn the wrenches, and the Reds began production, winning 70 of their first 100 games that season. Rose, Johnny Bench, Tony Perez, Lee May and Bobby Tolan contributed to a fearsome lineup that led the league in homers (191), batting (.270) and slugging percentage (.436). Rose collected 205 hits, not including his infamous crash landing into Cleveland catcher Ray Fosse that won the All-Star game at the newly-christened Riverfront Stadium. But in the '70 World Series, the machine conked out against the Baltimore Orioles' brilliant

Spotlight

To today's fans, Joe Morgan may be better known for his incisive analysis in the broadcast booth, but in the mid-1970s he was perhaps the most vital cog in the Big Red Machine. That speaks volumes, for the BRM was indeed a souped-up ride, featuring future Hall of Famer Johnny Bench along with stars Pete Rose, George Foster, Tony Perez and Ken Griffey. But Morgan made the engine whir. His clutch hits won Game 3 and Game 7 of the '75 World Series. He led the league in '76 with a .576 slugging percentage, and was named National League MVP in 1975 and '76, the first player since Ernie Banks (1958–59) to win the award in back-to-back years. Morgan won five straight Gold Gloves in the '70s and set a record for second basemen in '77, committing just five errors. Durability proved to be part of the Morgan package as well. He played for 22 years, and when he retired in 1984 as a member of the Oakland A's, he had belted 268 home runs, surpassing Rogers Hornsby as the alltime home run leader among second basemen.

In SI's Words

As a kid, Rose started out wanting to be a catcher, but by the time he was a high school sophomore he realized he wouldn't be big enough for that position so he took up second base. By 1965 he was a National League All-Star at second. In '66 Cincinnati Manager Don Heffner told him to move over to third.

"He didn't ask me, he told me," says Rose. "I moped around, which is something I never do, and I hit .170." Within three weeks he was back at second.

The next year, under Dave Bristol, Rose willingly turned over second base to his friend Tommy Helms and moved to the outfield, where he won Gold Gloves in 1969 and 1970. Then, one afternoon before a game early this May, he was breaking in a first baseman's mitt for his 10-year-old daughter Renee Fawn.... Rose was taking ground balls with Tony Perez at first, and Anderson said, "Boy, I wish you could take some of those on the other side of the field."

"I do, out in left," said Rose.

"I mean over at third," said Anderson. "I'd like for you to take a shot at third for me. I just need somebody to catch the ball and throw it over so Foster can play."

"Well," said Rose, "I'll try it...."

So Sparky tried Rose at third, a move that he has come out of smelling like frenchified after-bath lotion.

—Roy Blount Jr., June 9, 1975

Rose's headfirst slides (above), all-around hustle and pure intensity were an inspiration to his teammates; in the '76 Series Bench (right) hit a pair of home runs in the clinching Game 4, including a three-run blast in the ninth that put the game out of reach.

pitching and superb defense, losing in five games.

During a sub-par '71 season, the Reds came to be known as "the little red wagon," but they did acquire critical cogs George Foster, Cesar Geronimo and Morgan in trades. The Reds returned to the World Series in '72, only to lose to Oakland in seven tense games. Then in '73, Cincinnati lost a playoff series to the underdog New York Mets, before missing out on the postseason completely in '74. Whispers surfaced that the Big Red Machine lacked a key component: Heart.

After a 20–20 start in 1975, Anderson tinkered with the machine. In mid-May he moved Rose to third base, a position he had rarely played, and inserted Foster in leftfield, adding his volatile bat to the lineup. The Reds went 88–34 over the rest of the season and won the Western Division by a phenome-

nal 20 games, fueled by Morgan's .327 average and 67 stolen bases, which earned him the MVP award. The team so renowned for its offense sparkled on defense, putting together 15 straight errorless games. Four Reds—Morgan, Geronimo, Bench and short-stop Dave Concepcion—won Gold Gloves, and the Reds participated in one of the most dramatic World Series ever, against the Boston Red Sox.

In Game 6, at Fenway Park, Cincinnati fell victim to Carlton Fisk's legendary 12th-inning, game-winning homer, which tied the series. But the Big Red Machine bounced back in Game 7 when Morgan hit a two-out single in the top of the ninth to score the game-winning run. It was the franchise's first championship in 35 years. Still, nobody was prepared for the encore.

The '76 Reds are widely considered the greatest

team in National League history. Seven of their eight starters were selected for that season's All-Star team, and the other, Geronimo, hit .307 in the eight hole. The team led the league in home runs, triples, doubles, runs, batting average, slugging percentage, stolen bases and walks, and possessed the best fielding percentage. Seven Reds pitchers won in double figures. Rose led the league in hits (215), runs (130) and doubles (42), while Morgan led in slugging (.576) as he won the MVP for the second straight season. No game better displayed the power and self-assurance of the Big Red Machine than the one that took place at Wrigley Field on Aug. 11, when Cincinnati trailed Chicago 10–1 after three innings but rallied to win 13–10 in the tenth. The Reds played seven postseason games in '76 and won them all,

sweeping the Phillies in the NLCS and then crushing the Yankees in the World Series in a sweep never accomplished before or since. Cincinnati was also the first National League team to repeat as World Series champs since the New York Giants did so in 1922.

Howsam tracked down Anderson after the '76 Series and told him they had just watched the last great team either man would ever see. Indeed, the Reds would be the final ballclub to keep a core of magnificent players together before free agency transformed baseball into a game for transients and mercenaries, systematically dismantling even the Big Red Machine. "Looking back on that team is like dancing across the floor to Glenn Miller," Bench said. "You get that feeling of how it was when everything was so very good, the best...."

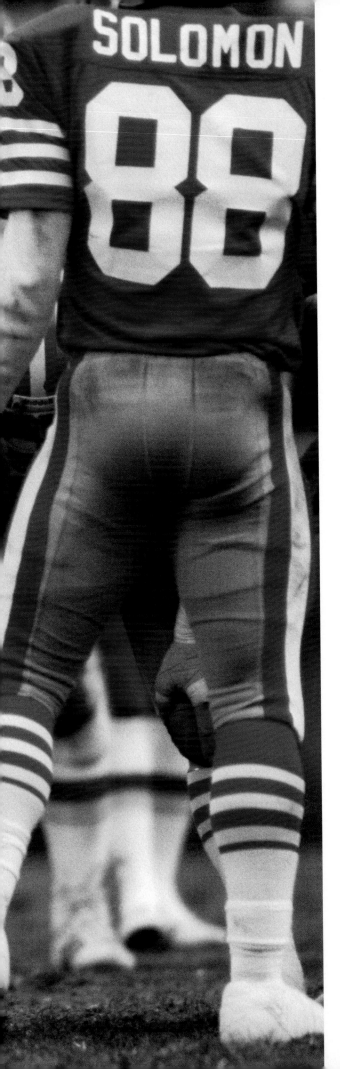

San Francisco 49ers

8

If imitation is the sincerest form of flattery, then consider San Francisco 49ers coach Bill Walsh positively beatified. Luckily for the 49ers, none of Walsh's many imitators has been able to orchestrate his confounding offense nearly as well as the inventor himself.

Beginning in the early '80s, Walsh revolutionized football with his "West Coast offense," an aggressive yet scientific attack that followed a carefully scripted game plan. While Walsh's offense has been run by some of the game's most talented players, San Francisco's long-term success can be attributed largely to the system itself. After all, during the '80s and '90s, the 49ers proved that you can replace parts—Steve Young for Joe Montana, Jerry Rice for Dwight Clark, Ricky Watters for Roger Craig, and even disciple George Seifert for Walsh—and the system will still crank out championships.

The West Coast offense has been so successful that it has migrated east. Eight other NFL teams have run variations of the attack since Walsh pioneered it. "I am a man who draws pass patterns on his wife's shoulder because my offense is how I gained my recognition," Walsh says. "I have watched it used by others with envy, even with a sense of plagiarism."

Walsh's inspired attack sparked five NFL championships for the 49ers from 1981 to '94. In an era of near parity in the NFL, the 49ers ignored the trend, remaining among the league's elite for as long as any team in NFL history. Over those 14 years the 49ers built a regular-season record of 159-56-1 (.740), went 19–7 in postseason play, won 11 NFC West titles and qualified for the playoffs 12 times, while enduring just one losing season.

Along the way the West Coast offense generated some extraordinary highlights. In 1980 San Francisco set an NFL record by

In spite of a shifting cast of characters around him, Montana (left) collaborated with Walsh for three Super Bowl wins.

rebounding from a 35–7 halftime deficit against New Orleans to win 38–35 in overtime. The 49ers averaged a humbling 30 points per game in 1984. The team won its three postseason games in 1990 by a combined score of 126–26, including a 55–10 rout of Denver in Super Bowl XXIV, the largest margin of victory and the most points in Super Bowl history. The 49ers also trounced Miami 38–16 in Super Bowl XIX and walloped San Diego 49–26 in Super Bowl XXIX.

Said Seifert, "There were times I walked the sidelines in awe of the way we were playing."

Hired in January 1979, Walsh inherited a San Francisco team that had played 29 seasons in the NFL without winning a single championship, the longest such drought in the league at the time. The 49ers had finished the '78 season with a 2–14 record and ranked dead last in scoring. Walsh gradually implemented what would come to be known as the

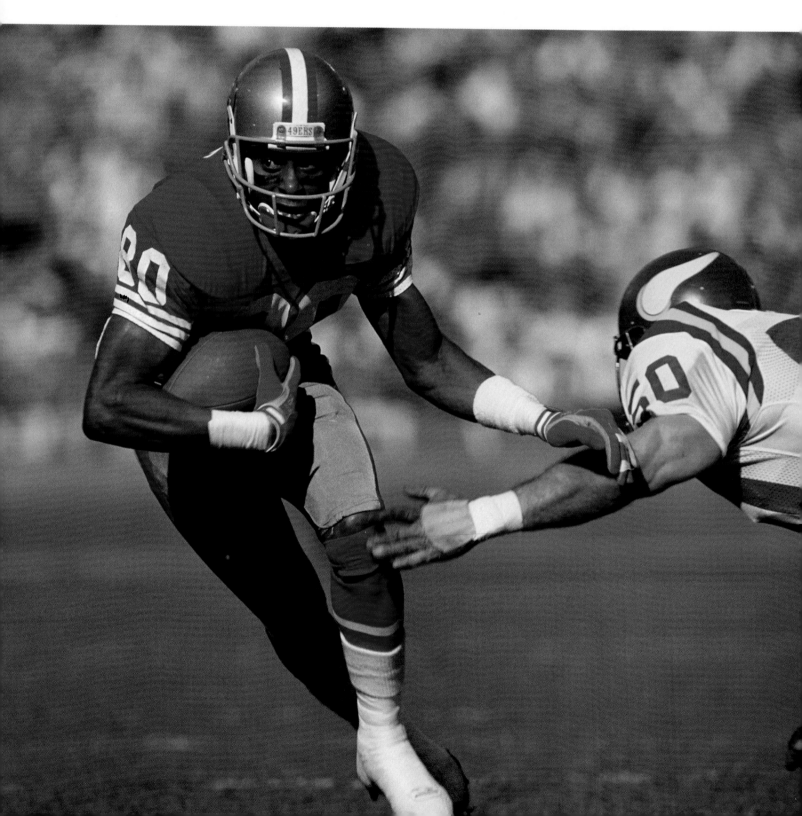

West Coast offense, and by 1981 the 49ers finished 13–3, becoming the first team since the '47 Chicago Bears to leapfrog from the league's worst record to its best in just three seasons.

Ironically, Walsh's era of supremacy began not with a precise 10-yard slant or one of his insidious throws to a running back flaring out of the backfield, but with a busted play. Trailing Dallas 27–21 in the final moments of the '81 NFC title game, Joe

Montana displayed the first real signs that he was becoming Joe Montana. After marching the 49ers 83 yards down the field, he faced a third down with 58 seconds left in the game and the ball on the Dallas 6-yard line.

Walsh called a "Sprint Right Option," but Montana couldn't locate an open receiver and quickly found himself retreating toward the right sideline. He lofted a pass that he later admitted was intended

Spotlight

As a high school kid Jerry Rice spent hour after hour catching bricks on hot summer days in Oktibeha County, Mississippi. Not ones thrown by a sub-standard quarterback in a pick-up game, but actual bricks that he was helping his father lay. "One of my brothers would stack four bricks on top of each other and toss them up. They might go this way and that, and I would catch all four. I did it so many times, it was just a reaction," he said. With all Rice has gone on to achieve as a wide receiver, it's surprising that high school coaches around the country haven't developed brick-catching drills.

But so much of what makes Rice great—nearly every NFL career receiving record bears his name—can't be taught. The moves he makes after catching the ball are as graceful as a ballerina's, and few have been able to keep up with his quickness off a cut. At crunch time he's the quintessential go-to guy. In 13 years with the 49ers, Rice never missed a game until he tore two ligaments in his left knee during the first game of the '97 season. Even if his career had stopped there, he would still have 22 more career touchdowns then the next guy on the alltime scoring list (Marcus Allen) and 3,684 more yards than the next player on the alltime receiving list (Art Monk). Add to those achievements a trio of Super Bowl rings and MVP awards for the '87 season and for Super Bowl XXIII, and it becomes clear why he is widely viewed as the greatest receiver of all time.

Rice (left), that rare combination of elegance and durability, caught more passes for more yards and more touchdowns than any receiver in NFL history; one reason for his success was the innovative—and now much imitated—offense of coach Walsh (above).

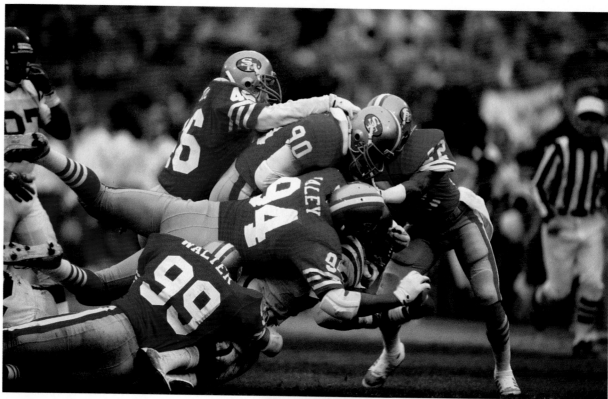

74

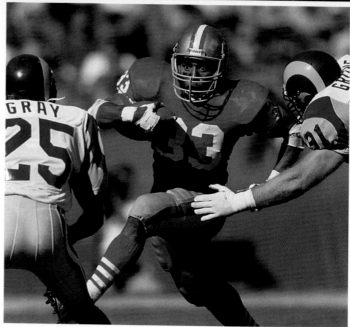

as a throw out of the end zone. But Clark, despite being weakened by a virus that had caused him to shed seven pounds in a week, sprung high into the air and somehow grasped the throw in his fingertips for the game-winning touchdown. "You get it from somewhere," Clark said. "How does the mother pick up the car that has her baby trapped?"

The Catch completely changed the image of a luckless franchise. Buoyed by Clark's heroics, Walsh guided the 49ers to a 26–21 victory over Cincinnati in Super Bowl XVI two weeks later. Over the next 13 seasons, San Francisco and its indomitable offense would collect four more NFL championships, giving the franchise more Super Bowl titles than any other in the NFL. The ballclub earned its reputation as the best football team of the modern era. "Who knows what would have happened to the 49ers if Clark doesn't catch that ball and we lose that game?" center Randy Cross said. "That win made it possible for us to get to the Super Bowl, not just that time but for years to come."

Said Montana, "It changed all our lives."

Even Walsh couldn't write a script that good.

With all the emphasis on Walsh's passing offense, it is easy to forget that the 49ers defense (top) was routinely among the league's stingiest; it is also easy to overlook the contributions of running backs such as Craig (above), who was a true all-purpose threat—in '85 he gained 1,050 yards rushing and 1,016 yards receiving.

Spotlight

Young (above) took over from Montana without a hitch, running Walsh's passing-oriented offense with astonishing efficiency; in Super Bowl XXIX he threw a record six touchdown passes and earned the MVP award.

As hand-offs go, the passing of the baton from Joe Montana to Steve Young had its share of off-field stumbles. There was no love lost between the two, and there were plenty of struggles over the starting spot. But when Young won Super Bowl XXIX after having watched from the bench as Montana claimed Nos. XXIII and XXIV, the relay team had to be declared a winner. With so many NFL teams battling mediocrity, San Francisco suffered for years from an embarassment of riches, with two MVP-caliber quarterbacks, and a third, Steve Bono, who would have been a starter on many other teams. Young and Montana racked up five regular-season MVP awards (Young two, Montana a record three) and are, respectively, the alltime Number 1- and 2-rated passers in history. In Young's Super Bowl start, he threw for a record six touchdown passes. Montana, who engineered four Super Bowl victories for San Francisco, was arguably the greatest comeback quarterback in history, with 31 fourth-quarter rallies, including a 92-yard drive in the final seconds of Super Bowl XXIII.

Los Angeles Lakers

9

The movement actually began many years earlier, in the early '60s, at a swinging L.A. nightclub called The Horn on Wilshire Boulevard. The Horn offered live music and comedy for celebrities and assorted wannabes. Jerry Buss, a wannabe real estate magnate himself, was a regular patron. Each night The Horn's entertainment commenced with a singer's belting out the club's trademark tune, *It's Showtime.*

Buss was thrilled by the pomp, the mood of anticipation whenever he heard that song, and he tucked away those memories until the day he purchased the Los Angeles Lakers in 1979. Looking to make his mark on his new team, Buss endeavored to capture the electric atmosphere of The Horn and transfer it to the fabulous Forum. He fired the Forum's organist and russled up a more lively band. He found himself some Laker girls. He invited every A-list celebrity he could think of to watch the Lakers, and gradually the Forum became its own scene. Buss, a Ph.D. in chemistry, had cleverly concocted his own version of Showtime. "I tried to create a Laker image, a distinct identity," Buss says. "I think we were successful. The Lakers are pretty damn Hollywood."

Buss had one chore left. He needed a dazzling

The arrival of the Armani-clad Riley in 1982 kicked Showtime into an even higher gear; when all else failed, the Lakers could always go to Abdul-Jabbar and his majestic skyhook (right).

team to match the glitz and glamour of the environ-ment inside the Forum. He needed some Magic. So Buss selected Earvin (Magic) Johnson first overall in the 1979 NBA draft, just months after the Michigan State sophomore had carried the Spartans to an NCAA championship.

Johnson was born to engineer the fast break offense that Buss so dearly craved. A 6' 9" point guard, Johnson could scan the entire court and instantly find a teammate with one of his flashy no-look behind-the-back passes for a spectacular dunk. A Lakers break directed by Johnson became the most

breathtaking stampede in hoops history, a sight so alluring that most of the teams in the Western Con-ference took on the same thoroughbred pace. Of course, Johnson was also agile enough to collect steals and wide enough to snare rebounds and occa-sionally, when all else failed, he might even try to score a hoop himself. Before long, the "triple-double" statistic was invented, the better to quantify John-son's unique talents. Said Julius Erving, "Magic's the only player I ever knew who could take only three shots and still dominate a game."

Erving first witnessed Johnson's talents when the

From his rookie sea-son in 1979-80 and his incandescent Game 6 performance in the Finals (right) to his years as the incomparable open floor conjurer (left), Magic remained as good as his name.

Philadelphia 76ers faced Los Angeles in the 1980 NBA Finals. After leading the Lakers to a 3–2 lead in the series, Kareem Abdul-Jabbar had to sit out Game 6 with an ankle injury. No sweat. Johnson punctuated his remarkable rookie season by substituting at center, scoring 42 points and grabbing 15 rebounds to clinch the series.

During the '82–'83 season Johnson spearheaded a clubhouse mutiny against Lakers coach Paul Westhead because he had instituted a half-court offense that did not allow Johnson to fully express himself. Enter Pat Riley, who favored a quick-strike offense

and a trapping defense that kicked Showtime into an even higher gear. Johnson led the league in steals that season and again guided L.A. past the 76ers for another NBA title.

After losing to an extremely physical Boston Celtics squad in the '84 Finals, Riley realized his team needed to rely more on its full offensive arsenal. Although somewhat obscured by all the Showtime antics, the Lakers could also run a devastating halfcourt offense. James Worthy possessed a solid mid-range jumpshot, Michael Cooper and Byron Scott could spot up outside and Abdul-Jabbar was

The Mountaintop

In 1978–79 the Los Angeles Lakers, with Kareem Abdul-Jabbar in the pivot, finished 47–35 and bowed out of the playoffs in the second round. Not a bad season, but hardly one that would suggest the team would be at the top of the NBA heap the following year. Yet that's precisely what happened in '79–'80. It wasn't smoke and mirrors that caused the turnaround. It was Magic. That's Earvin (Magic) Johnson, the sensational rookie who stood as tall as a forward but handled the ball like Curly Neal.

Fresh from leading Michigan State to the NCAA title over Larry Bird's Indiana State, Magic joined the Lakers and helped lead them to the NBA Finals against the veteran Philadelphia 76ers and future Hall of Famer Julius Erving. Then came Game 6 and Magic's defining moment as he brought the Lakers their first title of the '80s, taking over at center for Kareem Abdul-Jabbar, who had dominated the series up to that point but was sidelined with an ankle injury. Having eventually played every position on the court, Magic finished with 42 points, 15 rebounds and seven assists, earning the Finals MVP award along the way. As the NBA would learn over the next decade, the Magic act was just getting started.

always available down low for a skyhook. Abdul-Jabbar shot 60% from the floor in '85, a campaign in which all five starters shot 54% or better and the Lakers won 62 regular-season games. In a championship series rematch against Boston, Abdul-Jabbar averaged more than 30 points in L.A.'s four victories as the Lakers won in six games, exorcising the curse of eight previous postseason losses to the Celtics.

After Los Angeles defeated Boston again in the '87 finals, Riley realized he might need a new motivational strategy for the following season. With that in mind, just moments after the clinching victory he brashly guaranteed a repeat title in '88. The Lakers rose to the challenge, but not without an epic struggle. In the playoffs Los Angeles endured three consecutive seven-game series. In the deciding game of the NBA championship series against the Detroit Pistons, Worthy scored 36 points to clinch Riley's repeat. Los Angeles became the first NBA team to

In SI's Words

Last Sunday in Game 1 of the NBA championship series between the Celtics and the Lakers, Bird and Magic finally convened what had become the sport's most eagerly anticipated confrontation. From the moment the two of them walked onto the parquet floor in the Boston Garden—Bird solemnly pausing to grasp the bottom of each shoe with his hands to dry his palms, a ritual that makes him appear to be trying to remove chewing gum, Johnson flashing his ever-present grin—every move they made was studied, judged and compared on artistic impression and technical merit. When the game was over and the Lakers had won 115–109, with Magic scoring 18 points, taking down six rebounds and passing off for 10 assists compared with Bird's 24 (on 7-of-17 shooting), 14 and five, conclusions were quickly drawn and then hotly debated in the small hours from the corner bars of Brookline to the *boites* of Beverly Hills.

For the time being, both Bird and Magic have diplomatically kept out of the debate, but there's no doubt they've been paying attention....

—Bruce Newman, June 4, 1984

win back-to-back titles since the Celtics did in 1969.

The curtain fell on Showtime soon thereafter, but the Lakers had captured five titles in nine seasons. Los Angeles outlasted Boston to earn the moniker of Team of the '80s, an appropriate label, since the Lakers' high-scoring style symbolized the decadence and greed of the times. In just ten years, Buss had taken a cockamamie concept from a cabaret and created a basketball phenomenon, which is pretty damn Hollywood in itself.

The Lakers were a team of exceptional depth, including forwards such as Worthy (below), who could run the floor or stick the jumper, and A.C. Green (opposite), who provided the Lakers and Abdul-Jabbar with critical help on the boards.

81

He skated at age two. He signed autographs at 10. He demolished the NHL single-season scoring record at 20. He captured his first Stanley Cup at 23. It's a little more difficult to pinpoint at precisely what age Wayne Gretzky surrendered his identity, the exact moment at which he officially became *The Great One*.

Perhaps it was way back in a legendary pee-wee hockey game in Ontario, when a little kid named Gretzky stole a victory by scoring three goals in the last 45 seconds. Or during his third NHL season with Edmonton, when he set out to become the third player ever to score 50 goals in 50 games, but needed just 39 games to do it. Or maybe it was 1985–86, when he could have won the league scoring title with his 163 assists alone? All the numbers, a total of 56 regular season and playoff records, are so dizzying that they can't help but lose their relevance. Simply put, Gretzky is the greatest player ever to skate in the NHL, gifted enough to personally change hockey from a smashmouth game to one with its mouth agape. In the process he also transformed a grungy Alberta oil town into the glittering capital of the hockey world in the mid- and late '80s.

Of course, the Edmonton Oilers were more than just Gretzky. Much more. The Great One inspired many players around him to reach their full celebrity. Paul Coffey, Jari Kurri, Mark Messier, Grant Fuhr and Glenn Anderson all spent time sharing Gretzky's spotlight. These Oilers were so stocked with stars that the Hall of Fame may someday need a special wing just for them.

The line of Gretzky (99), Kurri (17) and Esa Tikkanen was simply the most productive in hockey history.

Edmonton's legacy is destined to revolve around its lethal offense, marked by unprecedented speed and creativity, while the team's goaltend-

Spotlight

According to Oilers' general manager–coach Glen Sather, when 18-year-old Mark Messier signed with the team in 1979, he was "no sure thing, but he could skate and he worked hard." Five years later, Messier was named playoff MVP for helping to lead Edmonton to its first Stanley Cup victory. With the series tied 1–1, the Oilers were down 2–1 against the defending champion Islanders when Messier skated the length of the ice and fired a rocket past Billy Smith, then the winningest goalie in Stanley Cup history. The Oilers went on to take the series in five games.

When Messier left Edmonton at the start of the 1991–92 season to join the New York Rangers, the 6'1", 210-pound center brought with him five Stanley Cup rings, one regular-season MVP award, one playoff MVP award and a reputation as a strong, swift skater and consummate team leader with a penchant for bruising fore- and back-checking. In his first season with the Rangers, he led them to a 50-25-5 record and the Patrick Division title with a 105-point total that earned him his second Hart Trophy as league MVP. But the Rangers came up short against Pittsburgh in the divisional final. It was a failure that would continue to haunt Messier until the 1994 postseason when he seemed singlehandedly to will the Rangers to their first championship in 54 years, scoring 12 playoff goals including the game-winner in the seventh game of New York's thrilling Stanley Cup final series with Vancouver.

ing and defense will always be underrated by revisionist history. It's just impossible to ignore all those goals. In '83–'84 the Oilers scored an NHL record 446 goals, or 5.6 per game. During that explosive regular season, Gretzky, Anderson and Kurri all scored at least 50 goals, making the Oilers the first NHL team ever to feature three 50-goal scorers. In the Stanley Cup finals the Oilers' tremendous firepower overwhelmed the steady Islanders in five games, ending New York's remarkable run of four straight titles. Gretzky scored four goals and had three assists in the finals to realize his childhood dream. "I've held women and babies and jewels and money," Gret-

zky said after that first title, "but nothing will ever feel as good as holding the Stanley Cup."

Gretzky vowed then to grab the Stanley Cup as often as possible. In the '85 postseason he scored 17 goals and set new standards with 30 assists and 47 points in one playoff year. Meanwhile Kurri broke a record with four hat tricks in the playoffs. Coffey shattered records for goals (12), assists (25) and points (37) for a defenseman. Fuhr posted a 15–3 record in the playoffs and stopped two penalty shots. Edmonton defeated Philadelphia in five games to win a second straight title.

The streak stopped abruptly in 1986, in the seventh game of the Smythe Division finals against Calgary, when Oilers

Messier (left) was just one of the players made better by Gretzky's presence; years later, playing for his sixth Stanley Cup, with the New York Rangers, Messier did the same for *his* teammates; amidst the torrent of scoring, Fuhr's acrobatic play in the nets (below) was often forgotten.

85

defenseman Steve Smith mistakenly shot the puck off Fuhr's leg and it ricocheted into Edmonton's net for the deciding goal. It is reasonable to assume that without that mishap the Oilers might have won five straight NHL titles—a feat unique to the Canadiens from 1956–60. In 1987 the Oilers defeated the Flyers in seven games and in '88 Edmonton swept Boston to win the team's third and fourth titles in five seasons.

At this stage Edmonton was still a young team. Who knows how long the Oilers dynasty would have lasted were it not for The Trade? That summer Edmon-

ton owner Peter Pocklington decided he could no longer afford his magnificent team, so on Aug. 9, he dealt Gretzky and two other players to the Los Angeles Kings. Most Edmonton fans can remember exactly where they were when they heard the news of what is considered to be the most significant trade in the history of American sports.

On the heels of Coffey's departure a year earlier, the Oilers regime was beginning to unravel. But, having struggled through the '88–'89 season adjusting to the void left by Gretzky, the Oilers made one final push in '89–'90. Messier

Willy Lindstrom (19), one of Edmonton's solid role players, was a member of the Oilers' '84 and '85 Cup-winning squads.

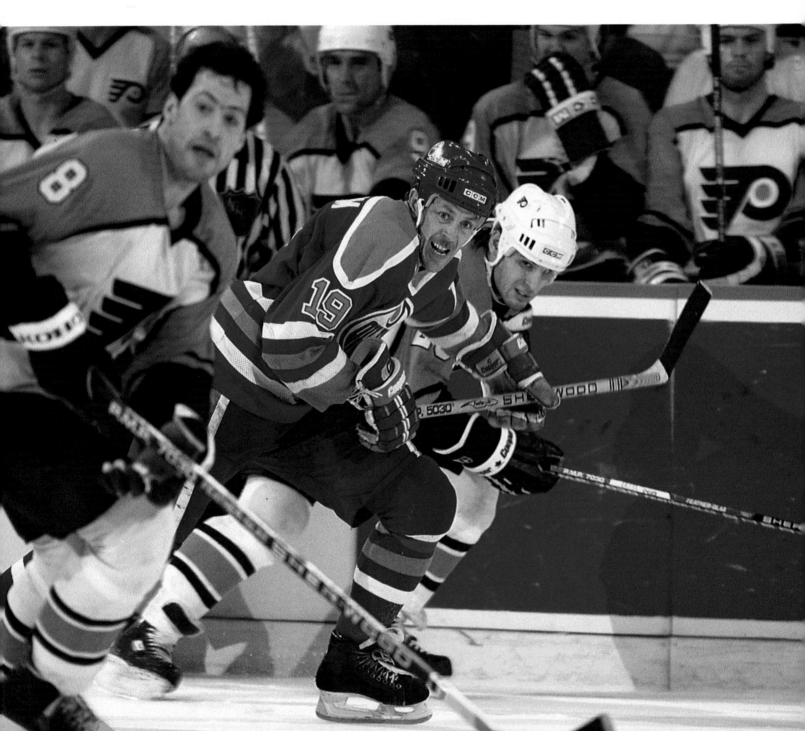

carried the team through the regular season and goalie Bill Ranford collected all 16 playoff victories as Edmonton defeated Boston in five games to win another Stanley Cup.

Seven Oilers, including Messier, Kurri and Anderson survived Pocklington's purge to capture five Stanley Cups in a span of seven remarkable seasons. That final title was particularly significant because it proved that Edmonton could win the Cup without Gretzky. Perhaps the proudest accomplishment of these Oilers is that their team came to be revered as more than just Wayne Gretzky, more than the Great One. The Oilers were the Great *Ones*.

The dark day that the Great One was traded by Pocklington remains etched in the memories of Edmonton fans.

Spotlight

If you were picking teams from a lineup of players based solely on physical stature, speed and strength, you would probably leave Wayne Gretzky for the other guys. At 6' and 175 pounds, he looks too delicate to be a bona fide hockey player. Indeed, in his early years in the league he was borderline anemic and usually finished near the bottom of the heap in strength and stress tests. The record books, however, tell another story. Gretzky has scored more goals than any other player in NFL history and holds a total of 56 individual records.

In attempting to explain his greatness, some have talked about his soft touch, others about the tremendous patience he uses to throw off defensemen. Opponents are awed by his seeming ability to move in several directions at one time, as elusively as an airborn feather. According to Bobby Orr, arguably hockey's alltime best playmaker, "He passes better than anybody I've ever seen." Ken Dryden, a former Canadiens All-Star goalie, said, "The thing about Gretzky is that unlike most other great goal scorers, he's a real sniper.... He doesn't miss much." After watching Gretzky anticipate the puck's trajectory off a teammate's missed shot, Phil Esposito, a brilliant goal scorer himself for the Blackhawks, Bruins and Rangers, commented, "That's why he's as great as he is. He's so smart." Perhaps the thing that most clearly marks him as hockey's greatest player ever, though, is his ability to bring out the best in teammates. "He knows where everyone is at all times," said former Blackhawk star Bobby Hull. "I could kick in 25 goals a year if I played with Gretzky."

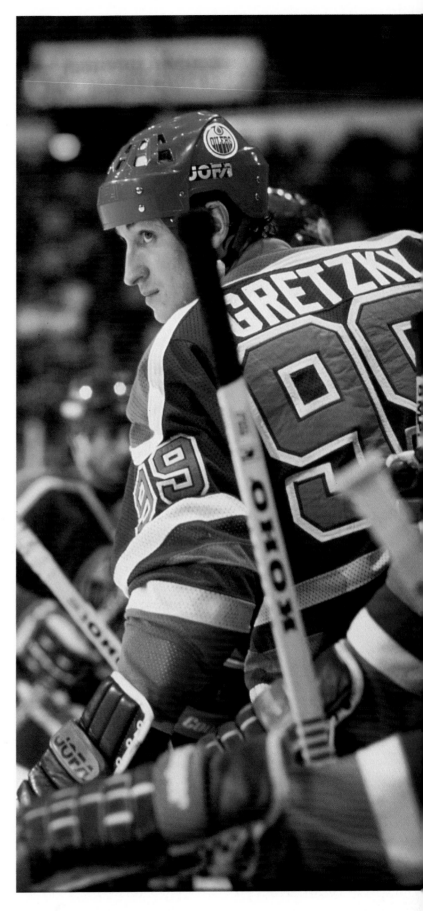

The innovative Brown (right), famous for shaking up the NFL's staid run-oriented offenses, beat the NFL champion Eagles in their second meeting without Graham throwing a single pass.

1946|55

Cleveland Browns

11

The National Football League welcomed the Cleveland Browns in 1950 with an unsettling glee. Sort of like ushering cows into the slaughterhouse.

From 1946 to '49, Cleveland had ruled the fledgling All-America Football Conference, building a 52-4-3 record and winning all four league title games by an average of 18 points. But the NFL teams were not impressed. They haughtily referred to the Browns as the champions of the bush leagues and itched to prove their superiority. Thus Cleveland's NFL initiation was personally arranged by commissioner Bert Bell, the former coach and owner of the Philadelphia Eagles, who scheduled the Browns' opener against the defending NFL champion Eagles. The game was played one day before every other NFL team began the season, in front of 71,237 raucous fans at Philadelphia's Municipal Stadium. It looked like a showcase. It smelled like a set-up.

Oops. Browns quarterback Otto Graham threw a touchdown pass in each of the first three quarters and ran for another score in the fourth period. Cleveland's slick receivers, Dub Jones and Mac Speedie, ran unabated through an overwhelmed Eagles secondary as Graham threw for a total of 346 yards. The final score read: Cleveland 35, Philadelphia 10. Afterward Eagles coach Greasy Neale said, "Jeez, they had a lot of guns."

Neale also indulged in some sour grapes, questioning Cleveland's toughness by harping upon how often the Browns had passed the football. So 11 weeks later, in a December rematch between the two teams, Cleveland coach Paul Brown pledged to run the ball more. The Browns won 13–7. Graham didn't throw a single pass.

The Browns finished the 1950 regular season 10–2, sparked primarily by running back Marion Motley, one of the first black pro football players, who led the league in rushing. In the championship game Graham tossed four touchdown passes and Lou (The Toe) Groza kicked a field goal with 28 seconds left to play as Cleveland defeated the Los Angeles Rams 30–28 to win its first NFL title in its first NFL season.

The NFL squads didn't know what hit them. To borrow some analysis from Greasy, Cleveland just had too many guns. Graham could throw his precise sideline and crossing patterns to Speedie, Jones and Dante (Gluefingers) Lavelli. Or Graham could hand

off to Motley, a bruising 238-pound rusher who averaged 5.7 yards per carry in his career and was also a devastating blocker. Motley ran behind three Hall of Famers on the offensive line in Frank Gatski, Bill Willis and Groza. On defense, Len Ford also reached the Hall of Fame as a pass rusher. And most important, at the controls Cleveland had Brown, the most innovative coach of his era.

With this talented cast, Cleveland won three more conference titles between 1951 and '53, but lost three straight championship games, the last two against

the arch rival Detroit Lions. After dropping eight straight games to the Lions, including the final regular season match in '54, Cleveland earned its revenge in the NFL title game. Graham, who had announced the game would be his last, threw for three touchdowns and rushed for three more as the Browns destroyed Detroit 56–10. Brown coaxed Graham out of retirement for one final season in '55, and Cleveland routed

Motley (left), among the NFL's earliest black players, averaged 5.8 yards per carry in his first NFL season; Graham

(below), rifle-armed and quick on his feet, may have been the first modern quarterback; both are in the Hall of Fame.

the Rams 38–14 to win the team's third NFL title.

Over the course of one brilliant decade Cleveland won 84.2% of its games, reached 10 straight championship games and won seven of them by an average of three touchdowns. It was hard to tell the Browns had ever left the AAFC. Even NFL commissioner Bell counted himself among the converts. Said Bell, "Cleveland is the best football team I have ever seen."

91

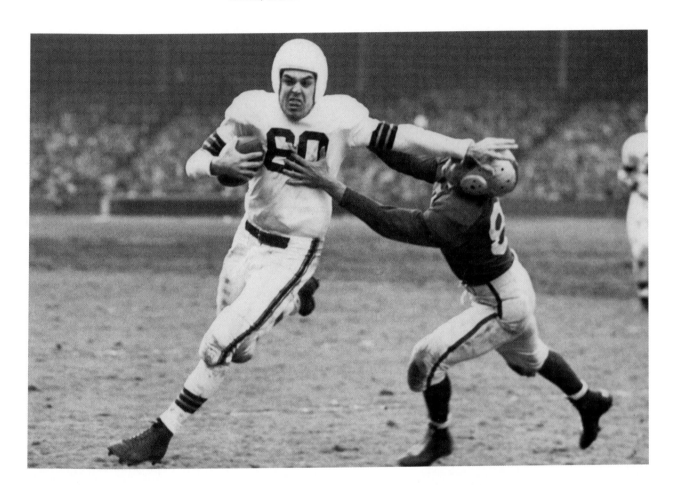

Spotlight

Otto Graham did not set out at a young age to claim more pro football championships than any other quarterback in history (four in the AAFC and three in the NFL). Au contraire. He was plucked from an intramural football game as a freshman music major at Northwestern and became a standout passer in three varsity seasons despite his desire to concentrate on basketball. When Paul Brown signed him to the Cleveland Browns in 1946, Graham had never played in the T-formation. But if Graham's ability to move between the oboe, the English horn, the piano and the violin was any indication, he would have no difficulty moving from tailback to quarterback. Indeed, he played the position with enviable calm and confidence, dodging linemen, or simply waiting a few beats, until he found just the receiver he wanted, then firing the ball with marksmanlike accuracy. Graham led the NFL in passing yards in 1952 and '53 and was inducted into the Hall of Fame in 1965.

The starters on the 1951–52 Lakers were (from left) Frank Saul, Vern Mikkelsen, Mikan, Pollard and Martin; they defeated the Knicks in seven games for the third of Mikan's six titles in seven seasons.

Minneapolis Lakers

12

One chilly winter night during the 1948–49 basketball season, the marquee outside New York's Madison Square Garden read, TONIGHT: GEORGE MIKAN VS. KNICKS. That was the perception of Mikan at the time. That all by himself this 6'10" behemoth could handle any other five men in short pants. Bring on the Lilliputians. Mikan was Hercules, Paul Bunyan, Goliath and Sasquatch rolled into one.

Everything around the Minneapolis Lakers center conspired to turn him into some sort of circus freak. Mikan's nickname was Scaffold, he wore an abnormally high jersey number, 99, and he appeared larger than life because his home court at the Minneapolis Auditorium was slightly smaller than regulation. The truth is that Mikan was not the only statuesque center in professional basketball at the time, just the only one whose agility complemented his size. He had an accurate hook shot with either hand and he was the best rebounder and shot blocker of his era. While the Lakers also had some more diminutive talent, such as Jim Pollard, Arnie Ferrin, Swede Carlson, and Slater Martin, Mikan alone symbolized the team. Fortunately for Minneapolis fans, Mikan played during a period in which a unique player, especially one who stared down upon almost everybody else, could dominate the entire sport.

Naturally, the rest of the basketball world plotted relentlessly to neutralize Mikan. Some opponents tried double-teaming the post, a tactic that had never been necessary before. The Fort Wayne Pistons froze the ball throughout a game in 1950 and won a snoozer, 19–18, to end the Lakers' 29-game home winning streak. In 1951–52, while the NBA was considering a 24-second clock as a means of stopping that stalling strategy, the league widened the lane from six to 12 feet, hoping to limit Mikan's powerful inside presence. Mikan still averaged 23.8 points per game that season and scored a career-high 61 points in a January game at Rochester.

Mikan was one of the original Lakers, and with him in the pivot Minneapolis was a championship contender from birth. The Lakers' bitter rivals in those days were the Rochester Royals, and in 1948–49 the two teams jumped in unison from the National Basketball League to the Basketball Association of America and finally in 1949–50 to the newly-created NBA, squaring off in thrilling duels

wherever they landed. The Lakers battled past the Royals in '48 and '49 on their way to titles in the various leagues. Then in '51 the Royals briefly interrupted the Lakers' streak of championships by upsetting them in four games in the NBA Western Division finals. Minneapolis rebounded to beat the New York Knicks in the '52 and '53 NBA Finals and then capture yet another title in '54 by beating the Syracuse Nationals in seven games.

After the '53–'54 season, Mikan complained of bad knees and retired at the age of 29 to pursue a career in law that would eventually land him a job as the first commissioner of the ABA. Mikan's departure marked

the abrupt end of the Lakers' run of titles and the start of a tailspin that would result in the franchise's migration to Los Angeles in 1960. The post-Mikan Lakers had trouble living up to Mikan's résumé, which included six titles in seven seasons and four NBA championships in the team's first five seasons in the league. However, Mikan's legacy extended beyond all the trophies he won in Minneapolis. He was professional basketball's first superstar drawing card at a time when college basketball ruled the hoops empire, and he is therefore credited with igniting the popularity that the NBA has enjoyed ever since. Mikan brought the callow league to new heights. Literally.

Contrary to popular legend, the early NBA players weren't nailed to the floor—Pollard (far left, 17) for one could jump and even Mikan (left) could get some elevation when necessary; his size and agility made him unstoppable under the basket, leading to nights like the one he and his teammates celebrated in 1949 (below) when he scorched the Knicks for 48 points.

Spotlight

If it had been left up to George Mikan's high school coach in Joliet, Illinois, basketball's first big man would probably have few titles to count other than the county marbles championship he won at age 10. And, if it hadn't been for the DePaul Blue Demons' coach, Ray Meyer, George Mikan would have headed for law school straight out of college. Luckily for hoop fans, Meyer realized "a big man could score more points by accident than a little one could trying hard," and began the transformation of Mikan from a friendly, physically awkward, bespectacled student into a fiercely competitive basketball player who threw countless elbows on his way to becoming the sport's first professional superstar.

Mikan led the Lakers to six titles in seven years. In the '49 championship series against Washington, Mikan played with a cast on his arm. "It fit right in with his elbows," said opponent Horace McKinney. "It would kill you. And it didn't bother his shooting a bit." In another playoff series, Mikan suffered a broken leg in a collision with another player. No matter. He played on it for three weeks. Over his career, Mikan shot .404 from the field and .782 from the line for 23.1 points per game while pulling down an average of 13.4 rebounds.

95

Apps (center), with Day (left) and Smythe (right) celebrated two Stanley Cup championships in Toronto.

Toronto Maple Leafs

13

Friends called Conn Smythe "The Little Major." Everybody else called him ... well ... never mind. The architect of the original Toronto Maple Leafs, Smythe was one tough soldier. During World War I he endured 14 months in a German prison camp. In World War II he was wounded while commanding Canada's 30th Antiaircraft Battery. World War III was any game Smythe's Maple Leafs played against the Detroit Red Wings. One night a Detroit fan hurled a chair in the direction of one of Smythe's defenseman, so the Toronto general manager hobbled down the aisle and slugged the patron into submission. Smythe's credo was blunt: *If you can't beat 'em in the alley, you can't beat 'em on the ice.*

When Smythe returned to Toronto from the Second World War, he was dismayed with the state of the Maple Leafs and set about rebuilding his proud team, which had reached six Stanley Cup finals in the '30s. His plan was to replenish an inexperienced club with veterans, as in *war* veterans. Smythe's blueprint began with a solid foundation, portly goaltender Walter (Turk) Broda, acknowledged as one of the best playoff goalies in league history. Smythe also penciled in young defensemen Jimmy Thomson and Gus Mortson, who would become renowned as the "Gold Dust Twins," as well as snipers Syl Apps and Ted (Teeder) Kennedy, the best two centers in the league. But perhaps the player Smythe favored most, the guy molded in the Little Major's own image, was winger Howie Meeker. After a grenade blast in World War II nearly shattered one of his legs, Meeker worked his way back into playing shape and scored five goals in one game in January of '47.

The '40s were particularly rugged times in the NHL, and coach Hap

Day's Maple Leafs were reviled as clutch-and-grab artists who thrived on instigating fights. It was this chippy yet effective style that helped Toronto capture the Stanley Cup in '47 as the prohibitive underdogs defeated the elegant Montreal Canadiens in six games.

Before the '47–'48 season, Smythe continued to upgrade his roster. He stunned the NHL by trading five of his Stanley Cup–winning players

With Broda in the nets (below), the Leafs won four titles in five years, including the 1951 championship, won when Barilko scored on a lunging backhander in the deciding fifth game (right).

to the Chicago Blackhawks in a deal for center Max Bentley. Smythe also unearthed 19-year-old defenseman "Bashin' " Billy Barilko, who would mature into the hardest hitter in the league. In the Stanley Cup finals, Toronto manhandled Detroit in four easy games. The Maple Leafs repeated their sweep of the Red Wings in the '49 finals as Broda allowed just five goals in the four-game series. Toronto's three consecutive NHL championships were

unprecedented, and they came as a particularly pleasant suprise to coach Day, a strict teetotaler who on this occasion indulged in a sip of champagne from the Stanley Cup.

After losing in the 1950 playoffs to Detroit, a team beginning its own run, the Leafs reestablished their dominance in '51. Toronto defeated Montreal in five games, all of which ended in overtime, to win their fourth Stanley Cup in five seasons. Barilko scored the deciding goal of the final game on a lunging backhand shot and was then hoisted onto

the shoulders of his teammates for a victory lap around the rink.

The 24-year-old Barilko was the crown prince of hockey and the centerpiece of Smythe's design for Toronto's future. But on Aug. 26, Barilko was on a fishing trip in the bush country of northern Ontario when his plane crashed, killing him and the Maple Leafs hopes as well. Smythe, who retired in 1961, never won another Stanley Cup, and Toronto didn't win another title for more than a decade.

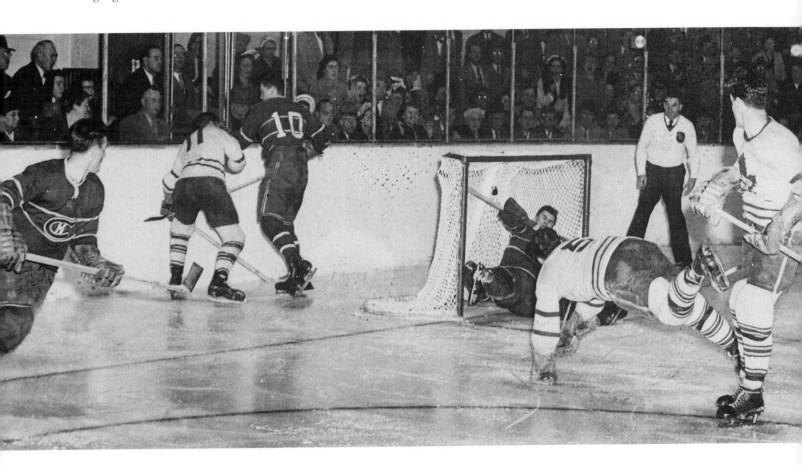

Aftermath

The Maple Leafs endured some lean years in the '50s, including four straight losing seasons at the end of the decade. But one of those campaigns, 1958–59, foreshadowed the upturn to come. Despite a regular-season record of 27-32-11, the '58–'59 Leafs made it all the way to the Stanley Cup Finals, where they fell to the mighty Montreal Canadiens. Toronto reached the Finals in '60 as well, again losing to Montreal.

In '61–'62 the Maple Leafs launched their second coming. Goalie Johnny Bower and high-scoring left wing Frank Mahovlich led Toronto to titles in '62, '63 and '64. The Leafs returned to the Cup Finals in '67 and upset the Canadiens of Henri Richard, Jean Beliveau and Yvan Cournoyer. They have not been back since.

The '70s brought a rebuilding effort and the emergence of Leafs Darryl Sittler and Lanny McDonald as NHL stars, while the '80s witnessed the nadir of the franchise, which featured a 20-52-8 season in '84–'85. Retooling in the '90s, Toronto acquired future Hall of Fame center Doug Gilmour, who led the Leafs to the conference finals in '93 and '94.

Also Greats

Also Greats

The teams in this final chapter bring a whole new meaning to the term "honorable mention." Somewhere Don Shula and his undefeated 1972 Miami Dolphins are saying to themselves, "Number 16? Are you kidding?" But those Dolphins are what this section is all about. They were an NFL supernova that arrived on the scene with an unprecedented flourish and faded almost as quickly. This chapter rewards the quirky teams, many of which come equipped with their own special asterisk, some undeniable caveat which makes them all the more lovable. The following pages provide a refuge where the cold-hearted process of counting championships sometimes gives way to less scientific judgment.

This chapter is a home for the Brooklyn Dodgers, one of the most talented baseball teams in history and a club that probably would have appeared among the Top 10 teams were it not for the New York Yankees. It's a place for the Los Angeles Lakers of Wilt Chamberlain and Jerry West, who in 1971–72 played on

Nick Buoniconti (85) and all his Miami teammates will probably take exception to the Dolphins' No. 16 ranking.

the best basketball team ever for a span of 33 games, all of which happened to be victories. It's a niche for the 1969-70 New York Knicks, who may not have been the greatest team ever, but were without a doubt the greatest *team* ever, and St. Louis's Gashouse Gang who set a standard for baseball hustle and overachievement that is still evoked half a century later to describe teams of a similar ilk. The chapter is a halfway house for the pugnacious Oakland/Los Angeles Raiders, who

won three Super Bowls while setting an alltime record for anarchy, and Charlie Finley's Oakland Athletics who won three straight World Series and finished a close second to their football neighbors in the turmoil department. It is also a haven for the underappreciated, such as the New York Islanders of the '80s, who quietly won four straight Stanley Cups, and George Halas's Chicago Bears, who captured four NFL titles in the '40s before most folks started paying attention.

Alas, plenty of deserving teams were left on the outside looking in. The Detroit Pistons' Bad Boys of Isiah Thomas and Bill Laimbeer, who won back-to-back NBA titles in '89 and '90 were the final team cut. Then there were Connie Mack's Philadelphia Athletics, who won the World Series in 1910, '11 and '13; the Toronto Blue Jays, who repeated as World Series champs in '92 and '93; and Mario Lemieux's Pittsburgh Penguins, who won back-to-back Stanley Cups in '91 and '92.

Among the other near-misses were the '66–'67 Philadelphia 76ers, who won a then-record 68 regular-season games, the brash New York Jets of '68, the miraculous New York Mets of '69 and Mike Ditka's '85 Chicago Bears, all of whom enjoyed one unforgettable season

Let's face it, writing this book was like sifting through the 50 Miss America candidates to find the top 30. The fact that Miss Rhode Island doesn't make the cut doesn't mean she isn't a lovely woman.

Our Also Greats chapter is a place for the Lakers of Wilt Chamberlain (left 13), whose team had one brief spell of brilliance, as well as Charlie Finley (right, middle) and his feuding A's, who dominated the early '70s in the American League.

1972 | 74

Oakland A's

14

Look beyond the Oakland Athletics' garish green and yellow costumes and those ridiculous lily white spikes. Look beyond the weekly middleweight title bouts in the clubhouse. Look beyond the absurd team mascot, a mule named Charlie O. Look beyond the absurd team owner, another mule named Charlie O. It is undeniable that the Athletics of the early '70s were incorrigible clowns, but they deserve to be taken seriously in spite of themselves. After all, those A's are one of only three teams in baseball history—and the only club with an address outside the Bronx—ever to win three straight World Series.

The blame for the Athletics' farcical reputation rests squarely with their megalomaniacal owner, Charles O. Finley, who treated his players like serfs and once tried to fire his second baseman for making two errors in a World Series game. But for all his draconian antics, Finley cunningly rallied a diverse mix of baseball ne'er-do-wells around a common passion: disgust for their owner.

That bizarre bond started to pay dividends in 1971, when Oakland won its first of five straight division titles with such building blocks as Sal Bando, Reggie Jackson, Vida Blue and Jim (Catfish) Hunter. In 1972 the underdog A's reached the World Series against Cincinnati and derailed the Big Red Machine with the help of Gene Tenace, an obscure backup catcher. Tenace, who had hit five homers all season, launched home runs in his first two Series at-bats and finished the Fall Classic with four homers and nine RBI. The Athletics outlasted the Reds in seven thrilling games, all but one decided by a single run. The most dramatic moment of the series occurred in the ninth inning of Game 2 at Riverfront Stadium, when Oakland's Joe Rudi made a magnificent game-saving catch against the leftfield fence.

The surprising Tenace was the star of the '72 World Series, hitting four homers and driving in nine runs.

The A's returned to the World Series in '73 and defeated the error-prone New York Mets in seven games, despite hitting .212 in the Series and sending 218 batters to the plate before finally cracking a homer in Game 7. Finley stirred up controversy when he tried to force his healthy second baseman, Mike Andrews, onto the disabled list after he committed two critical errors during Oakland's 10–7 loss in Game 2. Weary of Finley's meddling, Oakland manager Dick Williams resigned moments after his team clinched the championship.

Despite the arrival of evangelist-manager Alvin Dark in 1974, the contentious Athletics continued a rich tradition of intrasquad pugilism. The most infamous dust-up pitted Rollie Fingers against John (Blue Moon) Odom on the eve of the World Series, a bout that left Fingers with five stitches in the back of his head. "I believe the record is 15 stitches," Fingers joked afterward, "held by many." Oakland beat Los Angeles in five efficient games in the '74 World Series, the first staged entirely within the borders of California.

Two years later, recognizing the prohibitive expense of free agency on the horizon, Finley sold Fingers and Rudi to the Boston Red Sox and Blue to the New York Yankees for a total of $3.5 million rather than lose them without compensation. The deals were nullified by the commissioner in the interest of baseball, pushing Finley toward the baseball exit door.

He left a colorful legacy. Finley, who died in February 1996, once offered Blue $2,000 to legally change his name to True Blue. He offered his players $300 to grow mustaches. He campaigned for a switch to orange baseballs and multicolored bases. He wanted pitchers limited to three balls rather than four, and pioneered the idea of using track stars as designated runners. Finley once had relief pitchers brought out from the bullpen on mules. And he sponsored "Hot Pants Day." In summation, Minnesota Twins owner Calvin Griffith once said, "Finley's the P.T. Barnum of baseball."

To truly grasp the Athletics prowess, one must of course tune out the vast pandemonium of Charlie Finley's circus. Just focus on the three rings.

Finley offered Blue
(opposite page, left)
$2,000 to change his
first name to True;
Jackson (opposite
page, right) had as
contentious a rela-
tionship with Finley
as he later had with
George Steinbren-
ner; Rudi's catch in
Game 2 (left) was
one of the highlights
of the '72 Series.

Aftermath

The prickly Charlie O. eventually
sold or traded all of the stars of his
mid-'70s dynasty, and in 1979 the
A's hit an alltime low, losing 108
games and drawing a scant season
total of 306,763 fans to Oakland
Coliseum. Help came the following
year, dressed in denim. The Haas
family, owners of the Levi Strauss
blue jeans company, bought the A's
from Finley and set about restoring
past glory. They hired manager
Tony LaRussa in 1986, and invested
in their farm system, bringing
three straight Rookies of the Year
through the ranks: outfielder Jose
Canseco ('86), first baseman Mark
McGwire ('87) and shortstop Walt
Weiss ('88). The new owners bus-
ied themselves in the free agent
and trade markets as well, acquir-
ing pitcher Dave Stewart, outfielder Dave Henderson and
pitcher Dennis Eckersley. By moving Eckersley to the bullpen, Oakland gave him a new lease on his
career and, as it turned out, a
ticket to Cooperstown. The rebuilt
A's nearly equaled the success of
Finley's brawlers. They won four
division titles and went to three
straight World Series (1988–90),
winning one, in 1989.

15 New York Islanders

110 The red light flashed at 7:11 of overtime, but it wouldn't take a numerologist to figure out that the New York Islanders were a charmed hockey team. It was May 24, 1980, and Bobby Nystrom had just skated the length of ice, received a slick pass from teammate John Tonelli and executed a backhand flip over the shoulder of Philadelphia Flyers goalie Pete Peeters and into the net to clinch the first of a catalogue of Stanley Cups for the Islanders. It had been just eight seasons since the franchise entered the NHL as a comic expansion team. Just eight seasons since the maladroit Nystrom had been ordered by the Islanders coaching staff to take some skating lessons.

Nystrom, one of four original Islanders to capture that '80 Stanley Cup, symbolized the distance the Islanders had traveled in a relatively short time. After all, in the team's first NHL season, 1972–73, the Islanders endured a league-record 60 losses. When the Islanders visited Detroit one evening a banner hanging from the balcony read, THANK GOD FOR THE NIGHT OFF. Coach Al Arbour preached a sound defensive system and an offense based on the theory that "maybe someone would shoot it in off somebody else's butt and we'll win the game." In those undistinguished early days, general manager Bill Torrey often sneaked off the team bus to pay hotel bills personally in advance because the Islanders team credit was no good.

The turning point for the franchise occurred in 1975, when J.P. Parise scored a goal 11 seconds into overtime to defeat the despised New York Rangers and win the franchise's first playoff series. The Islanders would reach the Stanley Cup semifinals that year, and they continued to stalk a championship over the next few seasons, led by legendary line-

Bossy's arrival in 1977–78 marked the beginning of the Islanders rise; just three seasons later, he was hoisting the Cup (right) for the second time.

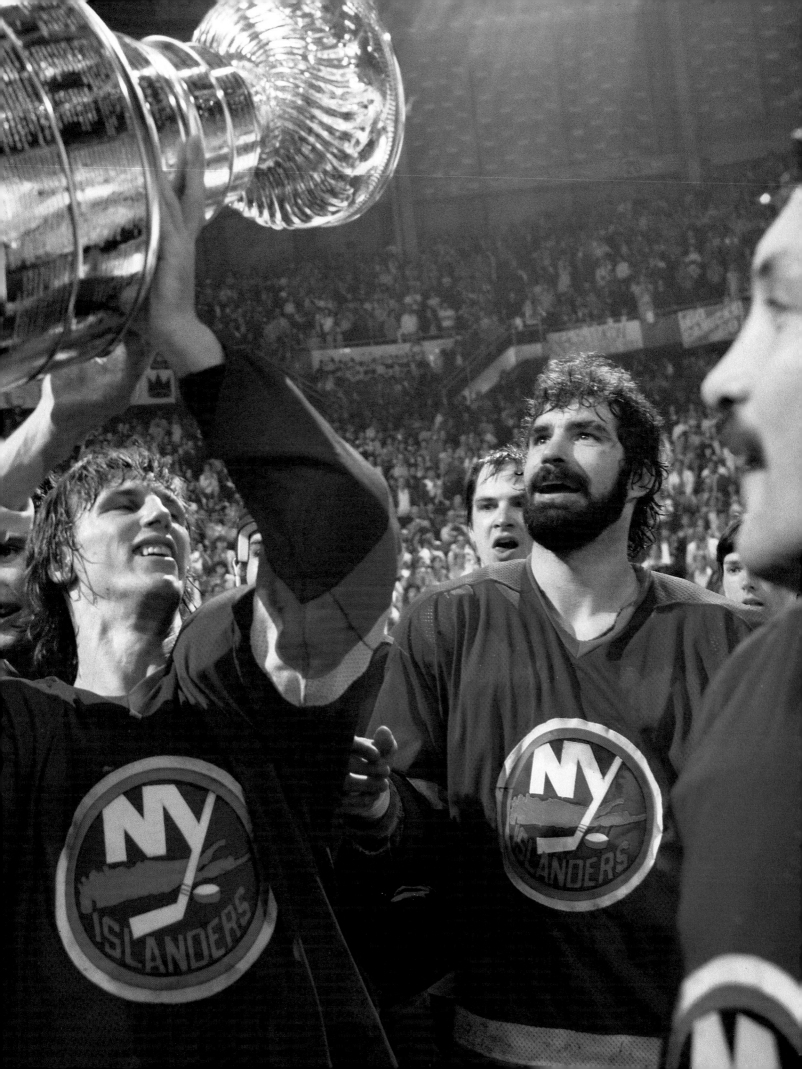

Bryan Trottier and Mike Bossy and rugged defenseman Denis Potvin, an eventual three-time Norris Trophy winner. In '78–'79 the Islanders mustered the best record in the NHL, but after suffering a bitter defeat to the Rangers in the semifinals they were considered playoff failures.

That was the final disappointment for a team which never lost its sense of humor. As the Islanders marched toward the postseason again in 1980, Clark Gillies regularly hid his teammates' underwear in the locker room freezer. Goalie Glenn (Chico) Resch once dressed himself at home in the dark and arrived at the rink wearing two different shoes. Early that season Billy Smith scored the first regular-season goal ever by an NHL goaltender. Then in March the team added two key ingredients: defenseman Ken Morrow from the gold medal–winning U.S. Olympic team and steady center Butch Goring, in a trade with the Los Angeles

Kings. The Islanders breezed through the playoffs until Game 6 of the finals reached overtime. As the Islanders prepared for sudden death, Nystrom sat in the locker room whittling a notch in his stick and then he proclaimed, "This goal is mine." Seven minutes and 11 seconds later, he backed up his promise.

The following season Bossy set out to score 50 goals in 50 games and accomplished the feat in dramatic fashion by scoring two goals in the final 4:10 of his 50th game. He scored 68 goals in the regular season and 17 more in the playoffs as the Islanders repeated as Stanley Cup champs by beating the Minnesota North Stars in five games.

Early in '82 the Islanders set an NHL record by winning 15 consecutive games, and they went on to sweep the Vancouver Canucks in the Stanley Cup finals, becoming the first U.S.-based team to three-peat. In the '83 finals the Islanders swept Wayne

The Isles were stingy in their own end, led by goaltender Smith (above), who was famously tough to beat in the playoffs, and defenseman Potvin (above, right), a three-time Norris Trophy winner.

Gretzky's Edmonton Oilers, temporarily delaying the birth of the Oilers dynasty.

Despite all their success, the fun-loving Islanders remained a small-town team in a big city market. The club was never feted with a tickertape parade down Wall Street's Canyon of Heroes like other champion New York area teams. Instead the Islanders celebrated with a spirited procession along the Hempstead (Long Island) Turnpike. Nobody complained. The Islanders were content, knowing they had finally earned some credit.

Spotlight

Nobody, not even Wayne Gretzky, releases the puck faster than Mike Bossy did. "I felt the quicker I got the shot away, the better chance I had to score," he said. "I tried to pick a spot, high or low, but other than that I didn't think about it. I just shot." And shoot he did. For nine consecutive seasons (1977–78 through '85–'86) he registered 50 or more goals for the Islanders, hitting the 60-or-more mark five times. After being passed over by 14 NHL teams in the '77 draft—they'd pegged him as a one-dimensional sharp-shooter—he set a rookie-record by scoring 53 goals. Bossy went on to become one of the best passers and play-makers in the league. Only in his 10th and final season did he dip below 50 goals, because of the back pain that would end his career. By the time Bossy retired, he had made eight All-Star Game appearances, earned a playoff MVP award in 1982, won the Lady Byng Trophy for sportsmanship three times and helped the Islanders take four consecutive Stanley Cups.

16 Miami Dolphins

17–0. The story could begin and end right there. Those numbers are why the Miami Dolphins occupy a unique and exalted perch in NFL history and will continue to do so until another team comes along and completes an entire season with a big, fat doughnut in the loss column. Look for that to happen about the same time that Miami freezes over.

Funny, just three years earlier, when Don Shula was introduced as Miami's new coach, he was very careful not to make any empty promises. "I am not a miracle worker," Shula said. "I have no magic formulas."

Call it what you like. Shula transformed a team that had finished 3-10-1 in 1969 into a 10–4 team in '70. The next season he engineered a 10-3-1 mark. At that point Miami really began to rewrite the history books. In an AFC playoff game against Kansas City on Christmas Day, 1971, the Dolphins battled the Chiefs in an epic saga that spanned nearly 83 minutes of playing time. Finally, Miami placekicker Garo Yepremian nailed a 37-yard field goal to give the Dolphins a 27–24 victory in the longest game in NFL history. Miami eventually advanced to Super Bowl VI, where the team still appeared drained and suffered an ugly 24–3 loss to Dallas. It was the last game Miami would lose for nearly 20 months.

The Dolphins began the 1972 season with a 20–10 win over Kansas City and won three more uneventful games before suffering their only significant loss of the season. Miami's quietly effective quarterback, Bob Griese, was knocked out in the fifth game with a broken right leg and a dislocated ankle and was replaced by 38-year-old Earl Morrall, who had been obtained on waivers from Baltimore. It's no coincidence that Shula's offense began to rely almost exclusively on its rushing attack, running behind a robust line that included future Hall of Famers

Csonka, the NFL's closest equivalent to a human freight train, was almost impossible for a single player to tackle.

116

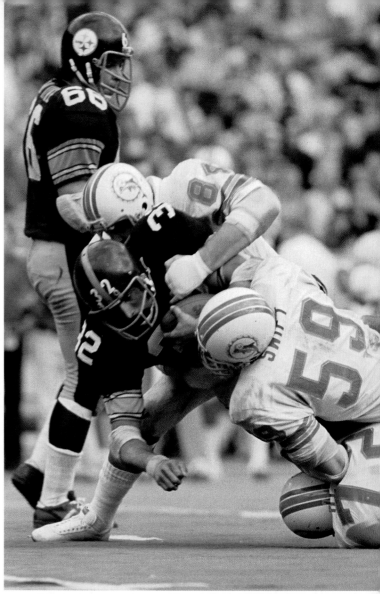

Jim Langer and Larry Little. Larry Csonka and Mercury Morris each rushed for more than 1,000 yards—the first time in NFL history one team could boast of having two 1,000-yard rushers in the same season—and the Dolphins broke the NFL record for rushing yards in a season. Meanwhile, Miami's No-Name Defense, led by Nick Buoniconti, Manny Fernandez and Jake Scott allowed the fewest points in the league. Miami played 1,020 minutes in 1972 and spent only 122 minutes and 51 seconds behind on the scoreboard. With a 16–0 shutout of the Colts in the season finale, the Dolphins became the only team ever to finish a regular season with a 14–0 record.

After defeating Cleveland 20–14 in the playoff opener, Miami edged Pittsburgh 21–17 in the AFC title game. Then, with Griese back as the starting quarterback, the Dolphins completed the perfect season with a clinical 14–7 victory over Washington in Super Bowl VII.

In the Dolphins' perfect season, Csonka, along with Kiick (far left) and Morris (right) shattered the NFL's single-season team rushing record, while Buoniconti (85, above) and the No-Name Defense gave up fewer points than any other team in the league.

Any dreams of another undefeated season were dashed by a loss at Oakland in the second game of the '73 season, but Miami still finished the regular season 12–2. The Dolphins easily defeated Minnesota 24–7 to win Super Bowl VIII—their second straight NFL championship.

Miami won the AFC East again with an 11–3 mark in '74, but lost to Oakland in the opening round of the playoffs. The following season the upstart World Football League robbed Shula of three major offensive weapons—Csonka, fellow running back Jim Kiick and receiver Paul Warfield—and Miami wouldn't win another playoff game until 1982.

Though Shula coached the Dolphins through the '95 season and became the winningest coach in NFL history, he never captured another Super Bowl, never again orchestrated anything like the "miracle" he pulled off in '72. All through that magic season, Shula steadfastly refused to acknowledge the historic trail his team was blazing. Finally, when the Dolphins arrived back at the Miami airport after Super Bowl VII, Shula relented. The coach raised the championship trophy over his head and addressed an enormous crowd of jubilant fans. "This is what it's all about," Shula said. "Seventeen and zero says it all. The greatest team ever in professional football."

Detroit Red Wings

17

Gordie Howe was once a goalie. As a 12-year-old at the King George public school in Saskatoon, Saskatchewan, Howe skated so awkwardly that he was placed between the pipes by varsity coach R.H. Tricky. Howe's team won the city title that year, but after the season he asked to switch positions. Why? Howe feared that continuing to stand still in an open-air rink in sub-zero temperatures might cause him to freeze to death. He had also decided that he preferred scoring goals to preventing them.

When Howe reached the National Hockey League just six years later at age 18, he skated so smoothly his critics griped that he wasn't really trying. He was also a confident marksman who could shoot the puck with deadly precision from his right or left side. On his first NHL shift in the Detroit Red Wings' 1946–47 opener, Howe was welcomed to the league with a jarring high stick that knocked out four of his teeth. He responded by scoring a goal in the second period, the first of 1,071 he would make during his 32-year career in the NHL and the World Hockey Association.

It didn't take long for Howe's enemies to discover that he was bigger, faster, rougher, dirtier and more competitive than almost any of them. He played what he called "religious hockey," meaning that it is better to give than to receive when it comes to stitches. Once, after receiving a stick check from Chicago's Stan Mikita that opened a cut under one of his eyes, Howe gave Mikita a sucker punch to the chin, then skated over to the wounded Blackhawk and said, "Did you get the number of that truck, Stan?" In another game Howe spotted his archrival, Montreal's Maurice (Rocket) Richard, breaking away toward the Detroit net. Howe leaped off the Red Wings bench

The Red Wings' Production Line of (from left) Abel, Howe and Lindsay spearheaded Detroit's run of four Cups in six seasons.

In SI's Words

"For Pete's sake, shoot, shoot!" Adams cried despairingly, one eye on Howe, the other on the second hand of the stadium clock. Again Howe held back his shot in favor of faking a defenseman between himself and the goal, and then took a lazy half-stride in the midst of which he flicked the puck low and hard past the Chicago goalie. The buzzer, signaling the end of the game, sounded a split second after the puck had bulged into the cords at the back of the net....Howe's unruffled, unhurried, Sunday-stroll-through-the-garden approach to the vigorous business of big-league hockey has periodically produced large lumps of anguish not only in the turbulent larynx of Jack Adams but also in the hearts of all good Detroit fans. Howe undoubt-edly possesses the completest natural talent of any modern hockey player, and what bothers the Detroit fans is the recurring dream of the prodigies he could perform if only he could light a fire under himself each time he steps on ice—as Maurice Richard of the Montreal Canadiens does without conscious effort, or, to name two others, "Teeder" Kennedy of the Toronoto Maple Leafs and Howe's teammate Ted Lindsay, "Old Forever Furious." In the meantime, they put up as best they can with Howe just as he is. For some he is, with Richard, one of the two greatest players in the game; for others, the greatest.

—Herbert Warren Wind, Jan. 24, 1955

and checked Richard off the puck, receiving just a minor penalty for his team's having too many men on the ice.

Howe (left, 9) was a master at using the boards to inflict punishment on opponents; Sawchuk (above, right) was a rock in goal for Detroit, winning the Vezina Trophy in 1952 and '53.

During the 1949–50 season, Howe, Ted Lindsay and Sid Abel came to be known around the Motor City as the "Production Line." The trio scored goals with factory-like efficiency, finishing that season as the league's top three scorers.

Still, in the opening round of the '50 playoffs Detroit had to face the Toronto Maple Leafs, who had won three straight Stanley Cups and had defeated the Red Wings in 11 straight postseason games. Playing without Howe, who had suffered a serious concussion in the opening playoff game, Detroit somehow extended the series to seven games. In a classic Game 7, Detroit's Leo Reise scored the match's only goal eight minutes into overtime. In the final series that followed, the Red Wings needed two overtimes in Game 7 before defeating the New York Rangers to win the Stanley Cup.

The Maple Leafs recaptured the Cup in 1951, but Detroit dominated the postseason in '52. With the help of the formidable Terry Sawchuk in goal, the Red Wings needed just eight games to plow through Toronto and then Montreal to win the Stanley Cup with an astonishing postseason sweep. Howe would carry Detroit to two more Stanley Cups, in '54 and '55.

Between 1949 and '55 the Red Wings finished first in the standings seven straight seasons and won four championships. After the 1954–55 season, Detroit general manager Jack Adams saw his team aging and decided to rebuild his roster, keeping just nine players from the previous season's Stanley Cup champs. It was a disastrous mistake. As suddenly as it had begun, the Red Wings' dynasty ended. Although Howe won six scoring titles before leaving Detroit in '71, the Red Wings did not win another Stanley Cup for 42 years.

18

Dallas Cowboys

The Dallas defense (above) was exceptionally quick as well as punishing; Aikman (right), the prototype contemporary quarterback, was big, agile and tough.

Does anybody still remember those dreary days in 1989 when Dallas became *Dallas*? The Dallas Cowboys were beginning to resemble the campy primetime soap opera of the '80s with Jerry Jones reprising the role of the oily J.R. Ewing. Jones purchased the team in Feb. 25, 1989 and later that day he unceremoniously fired noble Tom Landry, the only coach the Cowboys had ever known. Then Jones replaced him with Jimmy Johnson, his former University of Arkansas roommate and teammate, who was renowned largely for his heavily shellacked hairdo. Then the Cowboys finished that season with a 1–15 record, by far the most disappointing year in the history of the proud franchise. America's Team? Hah. The Cowboys weren't even Dallas's Team anymore. A bitter joke circulated around Texas Stadium during that season. *A woman drops off her three kids at Texas Stadium to watch a Cowboys game and they get lost. Later, someone from the stadium calls her and says, "Ma'am could you come get your kids? They're beating the Cowboys 14–3."*

Zealous Cowboys fans had no idea that the awful '89 season was all part of Johnson's master plan. His team's abject failure allowed the coach

to clean house, and he changed everything but the lone star on the Cowboys helmets. First, Johnson traded his most marketable commodity, Herschel Walker, to Minnesota for five veteran players and eight draft picks in what would eventually be viewed as the most lopsided deal since the acquisition of Manhattan. Then Johnson began rebuilding the Cowboys through the draft, selecting 15 starters in the drafts from '89 to '93. The key ingredients to the team's long-term success were receiver Michael Irvin, quarterback Troy Aikman and running back Emmitt Smith, who came to Dallas as three consecutive first round picks between '88 and '90.

After improving to 7–9 in Johnson's second season, the Cowboys put together an 11–5 record in '91 and reached the second round of the playoffs. The following season they finished 13–3 and won their first of five straight NFC East titles. After defeating Philadelphia 34–10 and then San Francisco 30–20, the Cowboys faced Buffalo in Super Bowl XXVII. Dallas forced a Super Bowl–record nine turnovers in trouncing the Bills 52–17. The next season Dallas finished 12–4 and once again advanced to meet Buffalo in the Super Bowl. Smith rushed for two touchdowns and the Cowboys won 30–13, to grab their second straight NFL title.

The Cowboys were stunned in '94, when a bitter

124

The Mountaintop

When the Cowboys ran roughshod over the Buffalo Bills in Super Bowl XXVII (52–17), the dread word—dynasty—was trotted out. Dallas was young, and the Bills were no ordinary opponent. Not only was Buffalo tough and tested, but it was making its third consecutive Super Bowl appearance and was due for a victory. But the Cowboys would not defer to age or experience. As individuals, they had overcome their share of adversity: Troy Aikman was born with a deformity of both his feet and had worn first casts then orthopedic shoes until he was three; Michael Irvin grew up one of 17 in a family so poor the children fought over food, beds and the single fan that brought relief from sweltering Florida nights. As a team, Dallas was running full tilt from an era of losing records and wasn't going to let a few Buffalos, no matter how big and battle-scarred, get in its way. With five minutes left in the first quarter, safety James Washington picked off Jim Kelly's pass, setting up a 47-yard touchdown drive. By the end of the game, Dallas's defensive quickness had forced Buffalo to commit nine turnovers— two were returned for touchdowns, three others set up touchdowns and another snuffed out a Bills drive in the end zone. And, yes, a great team, though perhaps not a dynasty, was officially born.

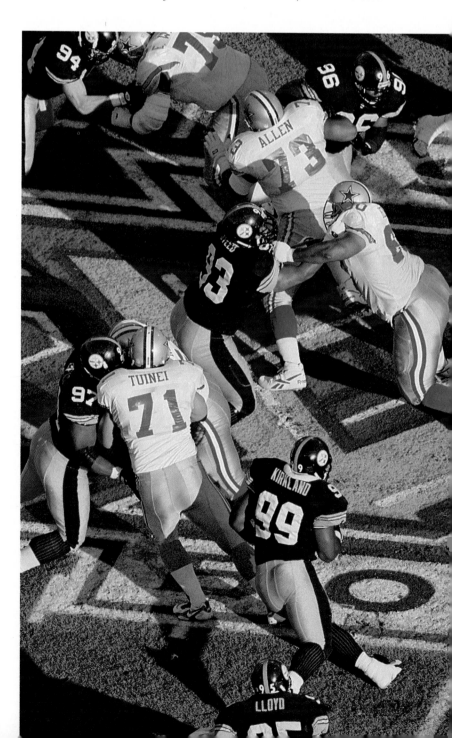

clash of egos between Jones and Johnson led to a quickie divorce and Barry Switzer was summoned to grab the coaching reins in Dallas. The team finished 12–4, but in the NFC title game against San Francisco the Cowboys fell behind 21–0 in the opening quarter and couldn't recover, losing 38–28.

Early in the '95 season Jones sparked his team by signing free agent Deion Sanders, who would prove dangerous as a cornerback, wide receiver and kick returner. While the '95 Cowboys didn't dazzle anyone during the 12–4 regular season, they found their stride in the playoffs. In Super Bowl XXX, Pittsburgh steered clear of Sanders and instead attacked cornerback Larry Brown, who intercepted two passes to help Dallas defeat the Steelers, 27–17, and collect another trophy.

A series of free agent defections and off-the-field legal problems eventually dulled the Cowboys' edge. But not before Dallas had become the only team to win three Super Bowls in four years. All the jokes and all the misery of Johnson's first season had given way to absolute satisfaction, an emotion best illustrated in the closing seconds of Super Bowl XXVII. Smith sneaked up behind Johnson and mussed his perfect hair, causing the Cowboys coach to giggle with joy.

Jimmy Johnson had the last laugh in Dallas.

125

Two of the Cowboys most potent weapons were Irvin (left), one of football's most dangerous receivers after he caught the ball, and Smith (far left) who ran for a pair of touchdowns in Dallas's 27–17 win over Pittsburgh in Super Bowl XXX.

A cold, egotistical, totalitarian tyrant, New York Giants manager John McGraw was widely known as "Little Napoleon," which could be an insult to the former emperor of France. For in ruling over the empire of major league baseball for more than two decades at the start of the twentieth century, McGraw may have been the most cantankerous figure in baseball history. McGraw's ballclubs played hard in his image, and so, despite being America's most recognizable franchise, they were generally scorned. The manager wouldn't have wanted it any other way.

Much of McGraw's hostility traces to the 1920 season, when Babe Ruth arrived in Gotham representing everything McGraw despised. While the Giants featured no matinee idols and therefore indulged in the strategy of baseball, Ruth's Yankees would shuffle around placidly until The Babe jerked one over the fence. McGraw had to share not only a city with the Bambino, but also a stadium. Both franchises played their home games at the Polo Grounds, which was owned by the Giants organization. Soon it became clear that the ballpark at Coogan's Bluff, vast though it was, couldn't contain both of them. So when the Yankees began to outdraw the Giants, McGraw did what any crusty slumlord would do. He served the Yanks with an eviction notice.

On May 14, 1920, the Yankees were informed that their lease would not be renewed following that season. Although the Yanks would hang around as undesirable squatters for two more seasons, this was the initial skirmish in what would become a bitter gang war.

With a foundation that included first baseman George (Highpockets) Kelly, second baseman Frankie Frisch, left-fielder Irish Meusel and pitcher Art Nehf, McGraw's Giants reached the '21

127

The Giants outfield included (from left): George Burns, who hit .299 in '21, part-timer Lee King, Ross Youngs, who hit .336 and led the NL in runs scored with 121 in '23, and reserve Vern Spencer.

World Series against the Yankees, a battle waged entirely at the Polo Grounds. Before Game 1, McGraw glared at Ruth and then barked at the Giants pitching staff. "Remember," McGraw said, "don't give that baboon anything but low curves." McGraw called every pitch thrown to Ruth in the series, and the slugger was limited to just one home run. Nehf pitched a 1–0 shutout in the clinching Game 8 as the Giants won the best-of-nine series five games to three.

The team that is generally regarded as the best in Giants history staged a rematch with the Yankees in the '22 World Series. Frisch and third baseman Heinie Groh combined for 17 hits, while Ruth batted just .118 as the Giants swept the series in four games. Nehf closed out the Yankees again with a complete-game victory.

The following year the Yankees finally moved to the Bronx and into brand new Yankee Stadium, setting up the first Subway Series. McGraw so detested the House That Ruth Built that he declined to have his players dress there, insisting that they suit up at the Polo Grounds and then travel to the Bronx in a fleet of cabs. Ruth hit three homers and scored eight runs to help the Bombers defeat the Giants four games to two. Perhaps realizing that he had lost his foothold forever, McGraw said afterward, "The old guard changes, but never surrenders."

The Giants won an unprecedented fourth straight pennant in 1924, but this time their arch enemies didn't show up. The '24 World Series, against the Washington Senators, lasted seven games. With one out and two runners on in the 12th inning of Game 7, the Senators' Earl McNeely hit an easy double-play grounder that hit a stone and bounced over the head of Giants third baseman Fred Lindstrom. The infamous "pebble play" allowed the game-winning run to score, a bitter defeat for McGraw, who would never reach such heights again.

Although McGraw continued to manage strong Giants teams, he never captured another pennant. After 30 years at the helm, he retired in 1932 and then watched from his centerfield perch at the Polo Grounds as the Giants defeated Washington to seize another World Series title in '33. Secure that the Giants could win without him, McGraw died four months later.

Aftermath

The New York Giants claimed the National League pennant four more times before decamping for San Francisco after the 1957 season. In 1936 and again in '37, late season surges earned them Subway Series berths. Unfortunately for the Giants, the mighty Yankees gunned them down 4–2, then 4–1.

It took the Giants 14 years after those World Series defeats to work their way back to the top—a spot they shared with the Brooklyn Dodgers at the end of the 1951 season. In the third game of the best-of-three playoff for the pennant, the Giants began the bottom of the ninth trailing 4–1. Two singles and a double cut the lead by one. The Dodgers brought in Ralph Branca to face Bobby Thomson, who promptly hit the "shot heard 'round the world." That earned the Giants another shot at the Yankees. Again their crosstown rivals prevailed.

Three years later, Willie Mays led the underdog Giants to a World Series sweep of the Cleveland Indians; it was the Giants' last season as a contender before leaving New York. In 1962, the San Francisco Giants and the Los Angeles Dodgers (who had headed west in 1958) staged a stranger-than-fiction replay of the 1951 postseason. The Giants again overcame a ninth-inning deficit in the third of three playoff games to advance to face—yet again—the Yankees in the World Series. They stretched the would-have-been Subway Series to seven before losing anew.

In a muddy football game against the Oorang (Ohio) Indians at Wrigley Field in 1923, Chicago defensive end George Halas snagged a Jim Thorpe fumble in mid-air at the Bears' two-yard line and returned it an NFL-record 98 yards for a touchdown with Thorpe in passionate pursuit every step of the way. The play represented a common theme in those days: Halas sprinting out ahead, and everybody else scrambling to keep up. The rest of the NFL would chase Halas for decades.

Papa Bear, who became slightly more renowned after concentrating his full efforts on coaching the Bears, came up with many football innovations still in vogue today, from daily practice sessions to pre-season training camp to studying game films. Halas coached NFL championhip teams at ages 26 and 68, but his Bears were most dominant between the Depression and the end of World War II. Halas molded those clubs into the NFL's original aristocracy.

Halas, who died at 82 on Aug, 5, 1991, is probably still upset that the first three contests in this remarkable Bears era all ended in unremarkable 0–0 ties. The team would endure three more ties that season, but Chicago still earned a place in the 1932 league championship game, which had to be played on an 80-yard field in Chicago Stadium because Wrigley Field was too snowy to be cleared.

In the NFL's first title game, the Bears defeated the Portsmouth (Ohio) Spartans 9–0, scoring the lone touchdown on a pass from Bronko Nagurski to Red Grange. As evidence that the league was still in its embryonic stage, Portsmouth's quarterback, Dutch Clark, the league's leading scorer, didn't play because he couldn't get time off from his job as a basketball coach.

Halas (middle, in Navy uniform) interrupted his military service to celebrate with his team after the Bears' 41–21 win over the Redskins for the 1943 NFL title.

The Bears repeated as champs in '33, scoring the deciding touchdown when Nagurski threw a halfback option pass to end Bill Hewitt, who lateraled to end Bill Karr for the final score in a wild 23–21 win over the New York Giants. Halas's Bears were a perfect 13–0 when they entered the 1934 title game against the Giants on an icy field at New York's Polo Grounds. Both teams slipped and sputtered through the first half, but during the intermission the Giants obtained some sneakers for better traction and they went on to whip the Bears 30–13.

Chicago played through the remainder of the decade without a single losing record but also without any more titles. The Bears regained their prominence by winning NFL championships in '40, '41, '43 and '46, though Halas missed the entire '43 season while serving as a naval reserve officer in the war.

From 1932–46, Chicago won six titles, the most memorable of them occurring on Dec. 8, 1940 at Washington's Griffith Stadium. The Bears had lost a regular-season game against the Redskins three Sundays earlier. In the interim, however, Stanford coach Clark Shaughnessy had answered a plea from Halas to help the Bears sharpen their new T-formation offense. With the attack clicking under the guiding hand of quarterback Sid Luckman, Chicago raced off to a 21–0 lead after just 13 minutes of play. At the end of the third quarter the score was 54–0. By the middle of the fourth, referee Red Friesel was down to the last of his allotted footballs, the others having been lost to specta-

Grange, star of the earliest Chicago teams and one of the key figures in attracting a fan base for the pro game, was still helping the Bears in the later years of his career.

tors on conversion kicks following the first 10 touchdowns. Therefore the Bears were forced to attempt a pass for an extra point after the final touchdown. In the end Halas's Bears squeaked past Washington 73–0, the largest margin of victory in any game in NFL history. In keeping with his demanding nature, the Bears coach wasn't completely satisfied. "Some observers said the Bears were a perfect team that day," Halas remembered years later. "I can't quite agree. Looking over the movies, I can see where we should have scored another touchdown."

Luckman, who engineered four titles during his tenure in Chicago, led the league in passing yards and TD passes in 1943, '45 and '46.

Aftermath

The Bears' 1946 NFL championship victory over the New York Giants (24–14) was Chicago's last title game appearance for a decade. In 1956—with George Halas on a two-year hiatus from coaching—Chicago again faced New York for the championship, this time losing 47–7. Halas brought one more championship to Chicago in 1963 before stepping down as coach for good four years later. With an offense fueled by Billy Wade's passing, future Hall of Famer Mike Ditka's catching and the rushing of Ronnie Bull and Willie Galimore, the Bears defeated—who else?—the New York Giants 14–10 for the 1963 title.

After spending most of the '70s and early '80s in or near the basement of the Central Division, Chicago went 10–6 in 1984, good enough for a shot at the NFC title. They lost 23–0 to the San Francisco 49ers, but the next season went a league-best 15–1; shut out the Los Angeles Rams for a Super Bowl spot; and beat the New England Patriots for the club's first title in 22 years. Halas was not there to see this one, but he had stuck around long enough to put the pieces in place: Coach Ditka, Walter Payton (the NFL's alltime rushing leader), quarterback Jim McMahon and hard-nosed middle linebacker Mike Singletary. Payton retired after the '87 season, but the team still made the playoffs in '88, '90, and '91 before slipping into a three-way tie for last place in the Central Division in '92. They lost in the second round of the '94 playoffs and have not been back to the postseason since.

21

1952 | 56   **Brooklyn Dodgers**

134   Sometimes it seemed like next year would never come in Brooklyn. In four straight star-crossed seasons, from 1950 to '53, the Brooklyn Dodgers twice lost pennants in the final inning of the final game of the season and twice won pennants only to suffer defeat in the World Series. At the bitter conclusion of each campaign, Dodgers fans from Canarsie to Flatbush to Red Hook chanted the same mantra: "Wait 'til next year."

It was the Dodgers' penchant for tragedy, combined with their fans' eternal optimism, that gave the franchise its sympathetic mystique. The team toiled inside America's coziest stadium, Ebbets Field, where spectators sat close enough to the diamond to hear the players' chatter. And players lived shoulder-to-shoulder with fans, returning to the same middle-class brownstones season after season. All this intimacy led the Brooklyn faithful to address their idols—and neighbors—as Oisk (Carl Erskine), The Duke (Duke Snider), Junior (Jim Gilliam), Pee Wee (Pee Wee Reese), Campy (Roy Campanella) and Newk (Don Newcombe).

The Dodgers were such an endearing bunch that *New York Herald Tribune* sports editor Stanley Woodward once groused that he regularly had to yank his reporters off the Dodgers beat because they lost their objectivity in the face of such a charming story. Roger Kahn, who covered the Dodgers in '52 and '53 for the *Herald Tribune*, paid romantic tribute to the team in his classic 1971 book, *The Boys of Summer*. Kahn took the title from a poem by Dylan Thomas, a tragic figure in his own right.

Campanella, Reese, Snider and Jackie Robinson were all future Hall of Famers, yet their fabulously talented team was affectionately known as Dem Bums, primarily because the Dodgers could not defeat the Yankees. "Those Dodger teams were among

A familiar sight: Snider being congratulated by Reese (left) and Gilliam (19) after a homer. Newcombe (right), **an intimidating presence on the mound, won 20 games in 1951, 20 in '55 and a league-leading 27 in '56.**

the best in the history of baseball," Yankees pitcher Vic Raschi said. "If the Yankees weren't the power-house they were, the Dodgers would have been the team taking eight of 10 World Series, the team hailed as the greatest of all time. They just had the bad luck of running into us all the time."

The golden era of the Brooklyn Dodgers—when the club reached the World Series four times in five seasons from 1952 to '56—couldn't begin until after the most recognizable moment of heartbreak in the history of the sport occurred, when Bobby Thomson of the New York Giants ended Brooklyn's '51 cam-paign in the ninth inning of the final game of the season by hitting a home run that would be dubbed

"the shot heard 'round the world." The next year the Dodgers finally did reach the World Series, but lost to the Yankees in seven games. In '53, Brooklyn fielded its best team ever and won 105 games. Cam-panella hit 41 homers and was named the league's MVP, Snider launched 42 homers, Robinson hit .329, Gilliam collected the Rookie of the Year award and Erskine won 20 games. Still, the Yankees dispatched the Dodgers in the Series in six games.

After an anomalous 1954 season in which nei-ther the Yankees nor the Dodgers appeared in the World Series, Brooklyn finally captured a champi-onship in '55, beating the despised Yankees in typi-cally heart-wrenching fashion. The Dodgers

A trio of greats (from far left): Robinson, who was a terror to opposing pitchers on the basepaths; Hodges, who hit 20 or more home runs 11 seasons in a row for the Dodgers; and Campanella, one of baseball's alltime greatest catchers, whose career was ended by a crippling auto accident which added to the sense of tragedy surrounding the Brooklyn franchise.

Spotlight

Imagine if Ken Griffey Jr., Bernie Williams and Kenny Lofton all played in the same city. New York baseball fans had a similar abundance of riches, and more, in the 1950s, when the Yankees lined up Mickey Mantle in center, the Giants boasted Willie Mays and the Dodgers fielded Duke Snider. It seemed they were always billed in that order too, with Snider bringing up the rear. But Snider hit more home runs in the '50s than Mays, Mantle or anyone else in baseball (326). Of Snider's fielding, rival slugger Ralph Kiner said, "I'd say Duke covers more ground, wastes less motion and is more consistent than anyone since DiMaggio."

While Brooklyn had its postseason troubles, Snider was no bum when the pressure was on. He had 10 hits in the '52 Series, four of them homers, tying the record then held by a couple of fellows named Ruth and Gehrig. When the Bums won their only Series, in '55, Snider hit four dingers again, becoming the only man in history to turn the trick in two Series. The Duke of Flatbush entered the Hall of Fame in 1980.

became the first team to come back from a two-games-to-none deficit to win the World Series in a best-of-seven format. Snider hit four home runs in that Fall Classic and Johnny Podres threw a 2–0 shutout in Game 7, a victory preserved by Brooklyn's diminutive leftfielder, Sandy Amoros, who made a tricky running catch in leftfield. The Dodgers were Bums no longer.

Order was restored in the final chapter of the rancorous Subway Series as the Yankees beat the Dodgers in the 1956 World Series, 4 games to 3. After the Dodgers lost 9–0 in Game 7, a new twist on a familiar lament rang out from the bleachers at Ebbets Field. "Wait 'til last year."

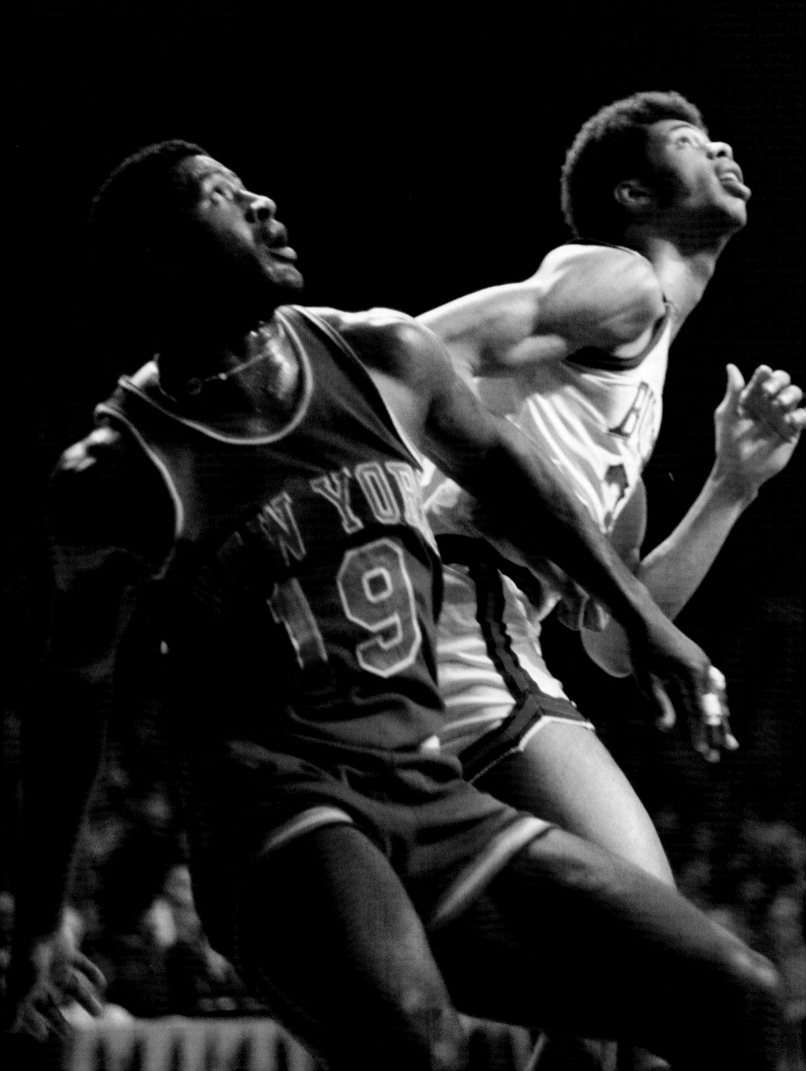

Before his unforgettable appearance against Wilt Chamberlain and the Lakers, Willis Reed (far left) had to deal with the Bucks and a young center then named Lew Alcindor; the Knicks' rise coincided with the arrival of the wily Holzman, who succeeded in convincing his team that unselfishness could be self-serving.

Bill Bradley was a Princeton alum and a Rhodes scholar who would become a Senator from New Jersey. Walt Frazier had a vocabulary by *Roget's*. Dick Barnett would earn a Ph.D. in business. Dave DeBusschere had already been an NBA player-coach with the Detroit Pistons and would later become the New York Knicks' general manager. Willis Reed would become a coach and general manager with the New Jersey Nets. Phil Jackson would go on to coach the Chicago Bulls to five NBA titles. Jerry Lucas memorized the Manhattan phone book. The Knicks of the early 1970s believed they were the smartest basketball team ever

assembled, and you'd have to be an idiot to argue.

Those Knicks were not the tallest, the quickest or the most gifted athletes. They were a team whose whole was far greater than the sum of its parts. A team which followed such corny textbook tenets as "move without the ball" and "hit the open man." And ultimately a team that understood that they could never win a championship by playing one-on-one. Said coach Red Holzman, "Those players were being selfish by being unselfish."

Concealed behind the veneer of teamwork, each of the five starters in 1969–70 did have his specialties.

Frazier was a creative play-maker and a master thief, Barnett a cocky streak shooter, Bradley a perpetual motion machine, DeBusschere a proto-type power forward and Reed an undersized center who made up for his lack of size with a patented fadeaway jumper. In that championship season, all five starters averaged between 14.5 and 21.7 points per game. "There was no go-to player," DeBusschere said. "Everybody was willing to take the big shot. It put a lot of stress on the defense."

The seeds for the Knicks' championship run were planted during the previous two seasons, with the hiring of Holzman and the acquisition of DeBusschere in a trade with Detroit. As soon as DeBusschere arrived the Knicks strung together eight straight wins and 12 consecutive victories at Madison Square Garden on the way to a team-record 54 victories. But in the playoffs the Knicks ran up against John Havlicek and the Boston Celtics nearing the end of their brilliant powers. After losing the sixth and final game of the division finals in Boston, which capped the Knicks' 14th appearance in the playoffs without winning an

Before Magic, there was the Pearl (left), the consummate court magician, capable of breathtaking spin moves and off-balance shots that some-how went in; if Monroe was off, there was always Frazier (right), the guard with ice water in his veins, who could stick the jumper from anywhere.

NBA title, DeBusschere walked around the sullen New York locker room murmuring, "Next year is ours."

The '69–'70 Knicks season began with phenomenal success. The team opened with five wins before losing a game to the San Francisco Warriors. Then New York embarked on an 18-game winning streak, an NBA record at the time, that pushed the Knicks' record to 23–1. The notion of an NBA championship in New York seemed more and more plausible, especially after local fans witnessed the underdog Jets capture Super Bowl III in January 1969 and the Miracle Mets win the World Series in October. In the NBA playoffs the Knicks defeated Baltimore and Milwaukee to reach an NBA championship series for the first time in 17 years. Reed strained a thigh muscle in Game 5 against Los Angeles and had to sit and watch Wilt Chamberlain score 45 points as the Lakers easily won Game 6 to even the series. But in an unforgettable moment in NBA history, Reed limped onto the court at Madison Square Garden just moments before the start of Game 7. He could barely run, but he scored four points in the opening minutes and the

Aftermath

After Willis Reed, Dave DeBusschere and Jerry Lucas played their last season with the Knicks, in '73–'74, the team began the long, painful process of rebuilding. Over 13 seasons they made it into the playoffs only five times. In the mid-'80s they suffered three straight sub-.300 seasons despite the arrival of lottery windfall Patrick Ewing, the Georgetown All-America center. Then, suddenly, they claimed the top of the Atlantic Division by going 52–30 in the '88–'89 season. But in a harbinger of things to come, they were downed by the rising Chicago Bulls in the Eastern Conference semifinals. Over the next four years, the Bulls eliminated the Knicks from the playoffs three times.

In 1993–94, with Michael Jordan in temporary retirement, the Knicks seized the moment and defeated the Bulls. After defeating the Indiana Pacers in seven games, they reached the NBA finals against Houston, where they fell in seven. The next year they blew a six-point lead with 18 seconds on the clock in the first game of the semifinals against the Pacers. Stunned and humbled, the Knicks lost the series. Their most memorable postseason disappearance, though, came in 1997. When the Knicks went ahead of Miami 3–1 in the conference semis, everyone expected that there would be yet another Knicks–Bulls faceoff. But when four Knicks left the bench in response to an altercation between Knicks guard Charlie Ward and Miami forward P.J. Brown, they earned automatic one-game suspensions, lost the series, and missed what may have been their best shot at stopping the Bulls and grabbing their first title in 24 years.

DeBusschere was a true power forward, capable of rebounding as well as scoring—he averaged 10.99 boards and 16.1 points per game for his career.

Knicks rode his inspirational wave to a 113–99 victory.

Amidst two seasons of bitter postseason disappointments, the '72–'73 Knicks strengthened their roster by adding Lucas and Earl (the Pearl) Monroe, two veteran players who longed to win a championship, having already achieved individual stardom. The Knicks crushed Los Angeles four games to one to win their second NBA title in four seasons. True to form, four different Knicks led the team in scoring over the five games. "In my heart it was the ultimate team," Lucas said. "There was no selfishness, no thought of individual statistics. The team always came first."

1926 | 34 St. Louis Cardinals

Just hours after St. Louis clinched its first-ever National League pennant with a 6–4 victory over the New York Giants on Sept. 24, 1926, Cardinals player-manager Rogers Hornsby returned to his hotel to find a telegram informing him of his mother's death. Hornsby thought back to the last time he'd seen her, already seriously ill, during spring training in Texas. She told him, "Your team is going to win the pennant this year, Rogers. I'll live until you win it." When Hornsby telephoned his mother's home after the Giants game, he learned that she had indeed lived long enough to learn of her son's monumental victory and that she had left a final message. *Win the World Series.*

That '26 World Series against the New York Yankees extended to seven games due in large part to St. Louis's 39-year-old pitcher Grover Cleveland Alexander, who won two of the first six games. Although Alexander had pitched a complete game in Game 6, Hornsby summoned him again in the seventh inning of Game 7 and Alexander nailed down a 3–2 Cardinals win that clinched the championship. The final out occurred when Babe Ruth attempted to steal second base and was tagged out by Hornsby.

By all accounts, Hornsby did not manage the most talented team in the majors in '26, but his club displayed by far the most grit, laying the foundation for St. Louis's similarly overachieving Gashouse Gang of the early '30s. Alas, Hornsby would not be a part of those Cardinals clubs. In the winter of '26, team owner Sam Breadon traded him to the Giants for Frankie Frisch, a transaction so unpopular in St. Louis that the Chamber of Commerce passed a resolution condemning it. Fortunately for Breadon, Frisch hit .337 in 1927 and fell narrowly short of winning the MVP award. Frisch then helped St. Louis win a pair

A trio of Cardinal pitching greats (from left): Dizzy Dean, 30-game winner in '34, Alexander, and Paul Dean.

Aftermath

If the 1931 Cardinals took the shortest flight path to the pennant, leading the entire season and finishing a commanding 13 games up, then the '34 team followed lead pranksters Pepper Martin and Dizzy Dean along the road with the most laughs. Their merry trajectory both on and off the field earned them the moniker Gashouse Gang, but it proved to be a hard act to follow. Although Dean threw for 28 wins in '35 and 24 in '36 the team wound up second to the Chicago Cubs and New York Giants, respectively, after late-season rallies.

A fractured toe in the '37 All-Star Game forced Dean to alter his delivery and ended his career as a Cardinal. After pitching four seasons for the Cubs, Dean took his braggadocio and penchant for malapropisms to the broadcasting booth, where, to the horror of the St. Louis Board of Education, he talked about batters striding "confidentially" to the plate, runners who "slud" into base and "empires" who made calls.

Early in the '37 season, player/manager Frankie Frisch removed himself from the lineup, no longer able to live up to his nickname, Flash. By midseason, Pepper Martin was the only player of note who remained from the '31 World Series team.

The trade of Hornsby
(far left) for Frisch
was an unpopular
one, but Frisch deliv-
ered to silence the
critics; Martin (left)
was the heart of the
Gashouse Gang, on
and off the field; Bot-
tomley (right) was
one of five future
Hall-of-Famers on
the 1931 Cards.

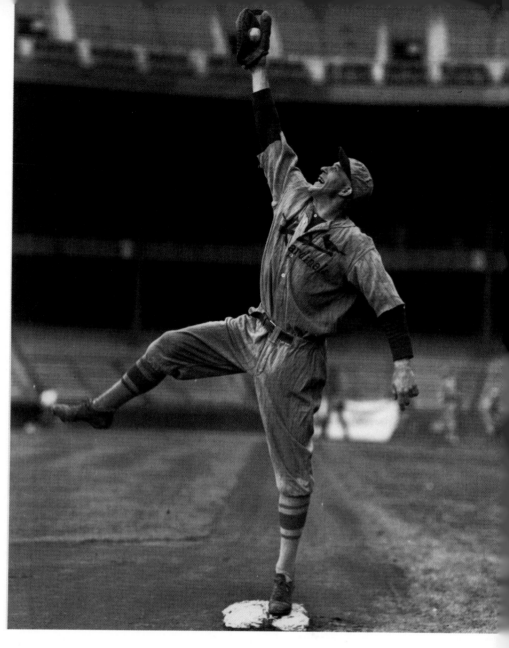

of pennants in '28 and '30, only to lose in the World Series to the Yankees and the Philadelphia Athletics, respectively.

If the Cardinals needed an extra jolt of inspiration, they found it in the arrival of Johnny Leonard Roosevelt Martin, a.k.a. Pepper, so named for his boundless spunk. The 1931 team included five future Hall of Famers— first baseman Sunny Jim Bottomley, Frisch, pitcher Burleigh Grimes, outfielder Chick Hafey and Martin—and it ran away with the pennant by winning 101 games. Martin was the star of the World Series against the Athletics, hitting .500 with 12 hits and five RBI. After St. Louis won the seventh game 4–2, Commissioner Kenesaw Mountain Landis congratulated Martin, saying, "Young man, I'd rather trade places with you than with any other man in the country."

Martin shot back, "That'll be fine, Judge, if we can trade salaries, too."

After two sub-par Cardinals seasons that led to Frisch's taking over as player-manager during the 1933 season, St. Louis captured yet another pennant in '34, fueled by the additions of shortstop Leo Durocher, outfielder Joe (Ducky) Medwick and a unique young pitcher named Dizzy Dean. The son of a sharecropper, Dean grew up picking cotton for 50 cents a day and didn't own a pair of shoes until he joined the Army. With Martin as his comic sidekick, the mischievous Dean regularly perpetrated pranks off the field and sometimes even cut up on the mound. He once brokered a bet that he could strike out Boston's Vince DiMaggio four times in one game. After striking out the first three times up, DiMaggio came up in the ninth inning and hit a foul pop. Cardinals catcher Brusie Ogrodowski settled under it until Dean screamed at him to let it drop. Dean struck out DiMaggio on the next pitch to win the 25-cent wager.

In 1934, Dizzy and his more subdued brother, Paul, dominated the National League, as Dizzy won 30 games and Paul another 19. In the World Series against Detroit, the Deans got all four Cardinals victories, including Dizzy's 11–0 victory in Game 7, while Medwick and Martin chipped in with 11 hits apiece. It was the Cardinals' third championship and fifth World Series appearance in nine seasons. Not bad for a bunch of underdogs so put off by the elitist attitude in the rival American League that Durocher once said, "They wouldn't let us in the other league. They would say we are a lot of gashouse ballplayers."

The Gashouse Gang was in a league of its own.

146

Looking at a black-and-white snapshot of a Detroit Lions game in the early 1950s, one can't help but wonder, *What's wrong with this picture?* Something's missing from the front of Bobby Layne's helmet. While all the other players wear either a single-bar face mask or one of the grills that would soon become commonplace, the Detroit quarterback's face is brazenly exposed. Layne was the last NFL player to compete without a face mask, and he carried his hubris even further by eschewing the customary padding for thighs, hips and ribs. Layne was no cowardly Lion. In the brash tradition of the Texas gunslinger, the Dallas-bred Layne believed that the only protection he required was a quick draw.

Layne was particularly cocksure in the waning moments of close games, during which he unwittingly invented the two-minute drill. However, nobody really recognized his discovery until the climax of the '53 NFL title game, when the Lions trailed Cleveland 16–10 in the final minutes. Layne stepped into the Detroit huddle with the ball set 80 yards from paydirt and said, "Aw right fellers, y'all block and ol' Bobby'll pass you right to the championship. Ol' Bobby'll get you six big ones."

Layne then engineered a masterful six-play drive that concluded with a 33-yard game-winning touchdown pass to Jim Doran, a converted defensive player, who hadn't caught a touchdown pass all season.

The other lethal weapon in the Detroit backfield at the time was Doak Walker, who shared a long history with Layne. The two players grew up just a few blocks apart in Dallas, and were teammates at Highland Park High. Layne played his college ball at the University of Texas, while Walker won the '48 Heisman Trophy at rival Southern Methodist before they crossed paths again in Detroit.

Layne (far right) and Walker (second from right) were boyhood friends in Texas whose paths crossed again in Detroit.

The Lions murdered the Browns. George Wilson, the quiet man no one knew very well, outcoached Cleveland's Paul Brown, who is regarded by quite a few people in the business as the best coach in football. The crippled Lions battered the healthy, rested Browns into a state of shock in the first quarter and kept them there for the next three. They played with the tough insouciance which is a trademark of this team, and they destroyed the poise of an opponent which had played the whole season with such calm efficiency. The men whom Buddy Parker had deserted in disgust because they could not be handled played brilliant football under the direction of Rote.

The Detroit fans loved it. Two men in the bleacher seats stripped to the waist and danced in the aisles, deliriously. Joe Schmidt, the wide, blond young man who is probably the best linebacker in football and who is also a co-captain of the Lions, was waltzed around the field on the shoulders of the fans for 30 minutes before he could escape to the dressing room. The crowd tried to break down the door to the Lion dressing room and nearly succeeded.

—Tex Maule, Jan. 6, 1958

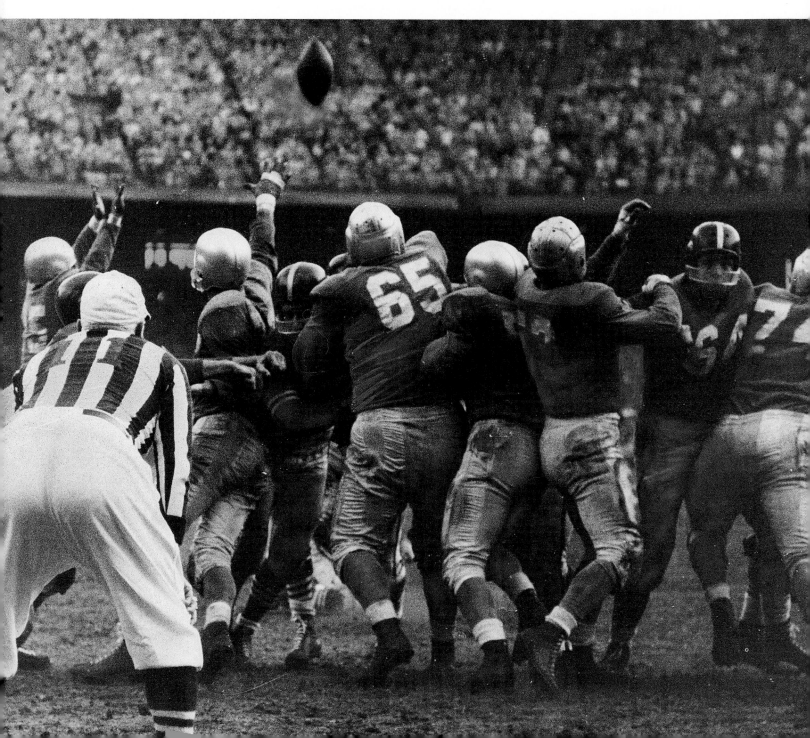

Some of the credit for Detroit's ascension must also go to coach Buddy Parker, who replaced Bo McMillin before the '51 season and took steps to simplify the team's maddeningly complex offense and defense. Parker basically handed Layne the ball and trusted him. In 1952 the Lions won eight of their last nine regular season games and then faced Cleveland in the title game. Layne scored on a 2-yard plunge and Walker added a 67-yard touchdown run and and the Lions defeated the Browns 17–7 for their first NFL championship in 17 seasons.

After the thrilling 17–16 comeback victory against the Browns for the 1953 NFL title, the two bitter foes met again in the final game of '54. Detroit imploded in a 56–10 loss to Cleveland that signaled the beginning of a Lions decline. Nearing the start of the '57 season, Parker sensed he had lost the respect of his players, and during training camp the coach

suddenly announced that he was quitting. Even though Parker moved on to coach in Pittsburgh, he continued to motivate his former team with the wakeup call he left behind. The rejuvenated Lions, under new coach George Wilson, went 8–4 in '57, but during the regular season's penultimate game the team lost the previously indestructible Layne for the postseason with a broken ankle. Backup quarterback Tobin Rote stepped in admirably, throwing four touchdown passes as the Lions destroyed the Browns, 59–14, to win the NFL title.

Two games into the '58 season Detroit traded Layne to Pittsburgh, where he was reunited with Parker. Detroit's will to win departed with him. The Lions won NFL titles in '52, '53 and '57, but none in the four decades since. "Bobby never lost a game," Walker liked to say. "Time just ran out on him."

Not before ol' Bobby got 'em three really big ones.

149

The Detroit defense (left) made it possible for Layne to perform his heroics; Walker (below against the New York Yankees) averaged 7.5 yards per carry and caught 32 passes for 564 yards in 1954.

On April 1, 1963, the Los Angeles Dodgers swept a generation clean by trading Hall of Fame outfielder Duke Snider to the New York Mets in a move that could have left the franchise looking like April fools. The significance of the transaction was enormous. The Duke represented the final spiritual link to the revered Boys of Summer, the lovable Brooklyn Dodgers team that had won the 1955 World Series. With Snider's trade to the Dodgers, the team had officially cut all nostalgic threads to their former turf in Brooklyn.

Or had they?

Sanford Braun grew up in the heart of Brooklyn—Bensonhurst—and was discovered by a Dodgers scout at Brooklyn's Parade Grounds while pitching for Nathan's Famous, an amateur team sponsored by the Coney Island hot dog company. By the time he joined the Dodgers in '55, he had changed his name to Sandy Koufax. Although his name appeared on the roster when Dem Bums finally captured the Series, hardly anybody noticed him.

Koufax spent his first six big-league seasons in almost total obscurity. He had a powerful left arm, but he couldn't find home plate with a compass. Koufax was so embarrassed about his lousy sense of direction that each spring he would work out in seclusion behind the barracks at the Dodgers compound in Vero Beach, Florida. Koufax was so wild that Snider once said that facing him

When Koufax (left) learned to control his wildness, he became one of baseball's best; what little help he got on offense came from Wills (below).

in batting practice was like playing Russian Roulette with five bullets in the chamber.

By the beginning of what would be a magnificent '63 season, however, Koufax had harnessed the amazing talent in his arm and was becoming the most dominant pitcher of his era—possibly any era.

Koufax collected 25 wins that season, including 11 shutouts, 306 strikeouts and his second no-hitter, and won the MVP and Cy Young awards. In the '63 World Series the Dodgers squared off with their archrivals, the New York Yankees, who had won six of the seven Series the two teams had played. The under-

dog Dodgers swept the Bronx Bombers in the greatest team pitching performance in Series history, highlighted by Koufax's record 15 strikeouts in a Game 1 win over Whitey Ford. In the four games the Yankees were limited to four runs and never held the lead.

After a miserable 1964 season in which Koufax threw his third no-hitter but also missed several starts with a sore arm, the brilliant southpaw once again dominated the sport in '65, striking out 382 batters. Koufax fanned 14 in a perfect game on Sept. 9 againt the Cubs. His unprecedented fourth no-hitter also highlighted his team's weak offense, which mustered only one hit and one unearned run in the game. Maury Wills led the team with an average of only .286 that season, but he often manufactured runs, stealing 94 bases. Meanwhile, pitcher Don Drysdale collected 23 victories, continuing his masterful career in the face of Hank Aaron's assertion that he was "the best spitball pitcher in the league."

The Dodgers and Giants squared off in a fierce '65 pennant race. In one game San Francisco's ace pitcher, Juan Marichal, grew enraged when Dodgers catcher Johnny Roseboro nearly hit him in the head with a ball he had thrown back to his pitcher. Marichal cracked Roseboro over the head with his bat, and Marichal's ensuing suspension cost him two starts. The Dodgers beat the Giants by two games in the final standings.

In the '65 World Series the Dodgers lost the first two games to the Twins, but came back to win in seven games as Koufax threw shutouts in Games 5 and 7. The slugging Twins, featuring Harmon Killebrew and Tony Oliva, who had been shut out just three times all season, were thrice blanked in the World Series.

Similar misfortune befell the Dodgers in the '66 Series against the Orioles. When L.A.'s Lou Johnson scored in the third inning of the opening game, it was the second and last run of the World Series for the Dodgers, who were swept in four games and shut out in the final 33 innings of play.

Having won 27 games and struck out 317 hitters that season, Koufax suddenly announced his retirement due to painful arthritis in his pitching arm. He had bowed out in the prime of his career, and in '72, Koufax, at the age of 36, became the youngest person ever elected to the Baseball Hall of Fame in Cooperstown, N.Y. "He left at High Noon," one admirer wrote, "a Hamlet in mid-soliloquy."

A remarkable era, in which Dodgers pitching alone won championships, left with him.

Drysdale (above) was intimidating on the mound, rarely allowing a walk and being more than willing to brush back opposing batters when necessary.

152

Spotlight

The great Dodgers teams of the mid-1960s were known for spectacular pitching and somewhat less than spectacular hitting. Their 1965 world champion edition batted a collective .245 with a league-low 78 home runs. Of course with the great Sandy Koufax and Don Drysdale mowing down opposing batters, Los Angeles didn't need much offense to win. Scraping together a few runs would do.

That's where speedy shortstop Maury Wills came in. In 1962, he had become the first player of the century to steal 100 bases in a season, finishing with 104, and he returned to that form in '65, swiping a league-leading 94 bases. That meant Will's singles and walks were as good as doubles. He also batted .286 that year to prove that not all Dodgers bats were anemic. In the World Series against the expansion Minnesota Twins, Wills was eager to make up for a poor '63 Fall Classic in which he hit just .133. His redemption came in the form of 11 hits, including three doubles, and three stolen bases as the Dodgers triumphed in seven games.

Atlanta Braves manager Bobby Cox advertised his team's remarkable achievement on a finger. Inscribed in a gold ribbon on the side of Cox's 1995 World Series ring are the words, *Team of the '90s*.

While that claim has yet to be rubber-stamped, rarely has one franchise dominated a decade the way the Braves ruled the '90s. As sexy headlines go, ATLANTA WINS DIVISION TITLE was right up there with SUN RISES IN EAST. In fact, next to the latter-day Braves, death and taxes seemed almost optional. From 1991 to '97, the Braves captured a division title every season, an unprecedented streak, since divisional play began in '69. No other team in either league has collected more than three straight crowns. Over that six-year span Atlanta's overall regular-season record was 79 games better than that of any other team in baseball. The Braves also earned six consecutive trips to the National League Championship Series and reached four World Series during those years. "Every spring it's almost a foregone conclusion that we're going to the postseason," pitcher Tom Glavine said. "You get used to things. Guys like me who were here when we lost 100 games need to remind the other guys that playing in October is not a God-given right. It's not in our contracts."

Indeed at the outset of the '90s there wasn't much positive karma in Atlanta. The Braves had not won a World Series since '57, when the team still played in Milwaukee. They had finished no higher than fifth place from 1985 to '90. In 1990 they finished in last place for the third straight season, having lost at least 97 games for the third year in a row. That season a section of lights fell into the centerfield bleachers at Atlanta-Fulton County Stadium. No Braves fans were in any danger of being injured.

Fortunately, all of those woeful

The Atlanta pitching staff, one of the strongest in baseball history, featured (from top): Steve Avery, Smoltz, Pete Smith, Maddux and Glavine.

155

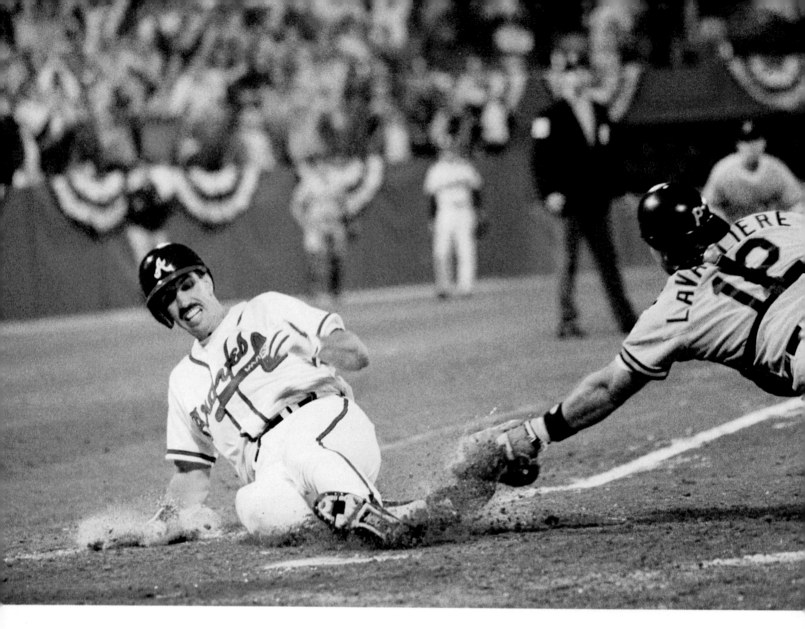

campaigns yielded prime draft picks which Cox, the Braves general manager in the late '80s, used to acquire stars such as Chipper Jones, Ryan Klesko and Mark Wohlers. The Braves left the rest up to the firm of Maddux, Glavine & Smoltz. Between '91 and '96 that trio of starting pitchers collected all six National League Cy Young awards. Greg Maddux captured four (one with the Cubs in '92) and Tom Glavine and John Smoltz won one apiece. The team's vaunted pitching staff was first or second in the major leagues in ERA every year from '92 to '97, and as the decade wore on, Young's name was invoked so often around Atlanta you would have thought he was the Braves' fifth starter.

The only criticism of Atlanta's reign is that despite all its success in those six years, the team captured just one World Series championship. So many brilliant seasons scarred by disappointing conclusions. The '91 Braves battled the Twins into the 10th inning of the seventh game of the World Series before losing a heartbreaking 1–0 contest. In '92 the Braves lost the Fall Classic to Toronto in six games. After losing to the Philadelphia Phillies in the '93 NLCS and enduring a baseball strike that canceled the '94 postseason, the Braves defeated the Cleveland Indians in six games to win the '95 Series. The following year Atlanta lost to the New York Yankees in the World Series, and in '97 the Braves lost in the NLCS to the renegade Florida Marlins. "You don't just snap your fingers and win a World Series," Cox said in 1997. "What we've created is a tradition of excellence, and you can't tarnish that by saying we've won only one World Series. Hey, we've been to four of the last six and we're not done yet."

Atlanta still had an opportunity to be regarded as a true dynasty, perhaps even the finest team in National League history. But to reap those accolades, Cox would have to accessorize some more of his fingers.

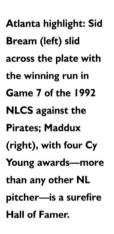

157

Atlanta highlight: Sid Bream (left) slid across the plate with the winning run in Game 7 of the 1992 NLCS against the Pirates; Maddux (right), with four Cy Young awards—more than any other NL pitcher—is a surefire Hall of Famer.

In SI's Words

What sets Maddux apart is an analytical, Pentium-quick mind that constantly processes information no one else sees. At home in Las Vegas he is a formidable poker player, detecting when an opponent has a good hand by the way he strokes his chin or suddenly stops fiddling with his chips. Maddux uses a numerical system in his head that tells him when to stand and when to hit at the blackjack table. But he is even better at analyzing hitters—so good that four times this year, while seated next to Smoltz in the dugout, he has warned, "This guy's going to hit a foul ball in here." Three of those times a foul came screeching into the dugout.

If his radar is that sensitive while kicking back in the dugout, imagine the clues he uncovers while bearing down on the mound. Says teammate Tom Glavine, the last National Leaguer to win the Cy Young Award before Maddux made it his personal property, "I think he's got a gift. He's able to notice things in the course of a game that no one else can—the way a hitter may open up a little, move up in the box an inch, change his stance. I've tried to be aware of that stuff. I really have. But I'm so focused on what *I'm* trying to do. I don't know how he does it."

—Tom Verducci, Aug. 14, 1995

27

Los Angeles Lakers

Jerry West's sneakers were so badly tattered that he had to tape the soles to the toes. Gail Goodrich insisted upon launching the final shot of pregame warmups and then grabbing a towel from the team trainer, which he superstitiously tossed on the floor. Coach Bill Sharman kept two pens clipped to his inside coat pocket, then compulsively switched them to his shirt pocket right before tip-off. One night, Dorothy Sharman, his wife and good luck charm, tried to beg out of a Lakers game with a 101-degree temperature, but the coach dragged her to the contest anyway so as not to jeopardize The Streak.

O.K., so they obsessed a little. But the mighty Los Angeles Lakers did not lose an NBA basketball game between Oct. 31, 1971 and Jan. 9, 1972. The Streak encompassed an NBA-record 33 consecutive victories and a full 70 days. The monumental string began just as the franchise was mourning the loss of Hall of Fame forward Elgin Baylor, who surrendered to his brittle knees and announced his retirement on Oct. 30. It included 16 victories at home and 17 on the road. The Lakers won in Boston. They won in Baltimore. They won in overtime against Phoenix. And they won by 44 points in Atlanta for the last victory in the streak. When the Lakers finally succumbed to defending champion Milwaukee and Kareem Abdul-Jabbar, L.A. had set a new standard not merely for basketball, but for all major pro sports. The feat was so mind-boggling that Wilt Chamberlain had begun facetiously comparing it to the time he won 445 straight games with the Harlem Globetrotters. "During the streak we knew before we walked out onto the court that we were going to win," forward Jim McMillian said, "and the other team knew it, too."

The Lakers had started an amazing yet frustrating championship crusade in '61–'62, when they lost to Boston in the

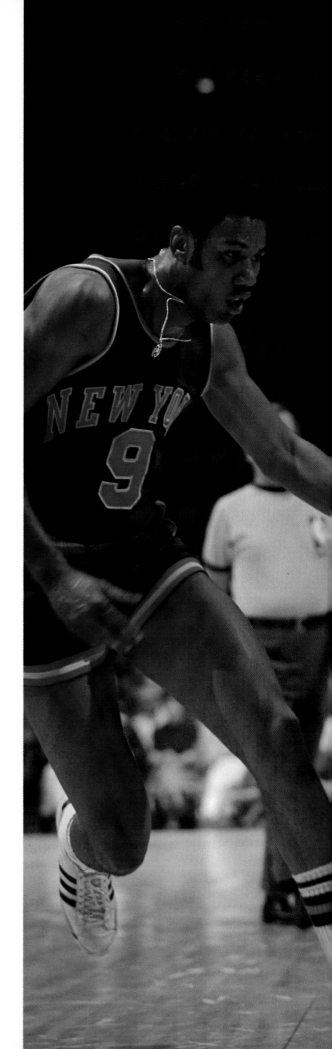

West (with ball), the league's purest shooter and one of its finest playmakers, averaged 25.8 points per game and led the league in assists in '71–'72.

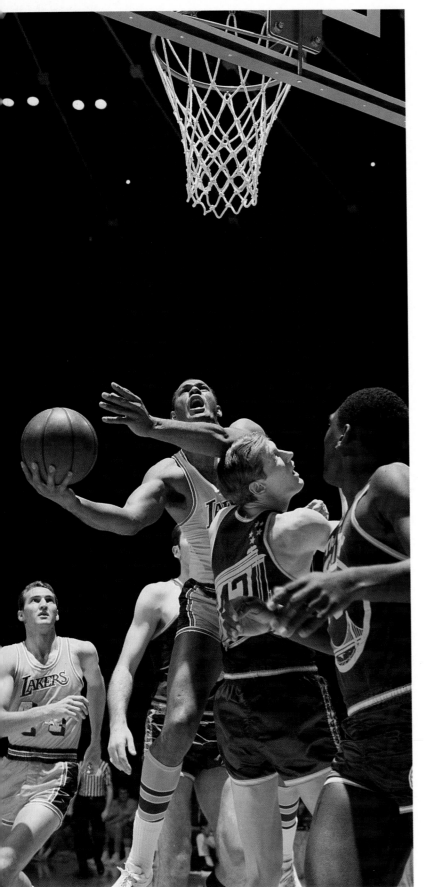

In SI's Words

Guard Keith Erickson of the Los Angeles Lakers ambled out onto the court with his teammates to warm up for an exhibition game one night last week and Seattle Coach Al Bianchi called out to him: "Hey Keith, who's that new guy you got with the beard?"

The new guy was Wilt Chamberlain, the man who once scored 100 points in a regulation NBA game, the man who once took 55 rebounds against the Boston Celtics. He is now a Laker, joining Elgin Baylor and Jerry West to make L.A.—on paper anyway—the greatest basketball team ever. Of the five best pros playing today—Wilt, Elgin, Jerry, Oscar Robertson and Bill Russell—the Lakers this season have three. The trade that sent Chamberlain from the Philadelphia 76ers to L.A. (to continue this season of sweeping statements) must rank close to the top of the most astounding deals in the history of professional sport. It is as if the Niblets people traded the Jolly Green Giant to Heinz for a soup recipe and two vats of pickles.

—Joe Jares, Oct. 14, 1968

NBA finals. Over the next 11 seasons L.A. would return to the finals eight times. Alas, the Lakers would lose seven of those series, including five to the rival Celtics.

Nobody in Los Angeles really believed the Lakers could win a title until a 1968 trade brought Chamberlain to the Lakers, giving the team three NBA legends among the club's starting five. Chamberlain averaged 20.5 points and 21.1 rebounds in his first Lakers season, and Los Angeles once again faced Boston in the finals, this time as the favorites. But the Celtics scratched out a 108–106 victory in Game 7 to dash the Lakers' hopes again.

After losing the 1970 finals in seven games to the Knicks and bowing out against Milwaukee in the '71 conference finals, Lakers owner Jack Kent Cooke shuffled his coaching staff before the '71–'72 season, hiring Sharman as head coach and K.C. Jones as an assistant in the hope that two Celtics alums could befuddle their former team. Sharman appointed the mercurial Chamberlain team captain and set about trying to turn him into Bill Russell. He asked the Big Dipper to concentrate on rebounds and blocked shots, and the game's most prolific scorer led the

Sadly for the great Baylor (with ball), he retired before the streak began and missed the title that followed it as well.

NBA with 19.2 rebounds per game. Sharman asked West, the league's purest
jump shooter, to focus more on playmak-
ing, and West led the league in assists.
Meanwhile, Goodrich filled the scoring
void by averaging 25.9 points per game.
Buoyed by the streak, the Lakers won a
record 69 games in the regular season,
routing their opponents by an average of 12.3 points
per game. But the team was still hungry for that
elusive title. Having dispatched Chicago and Milwaukee to reach yet another NBA finals, Los Angeles defeated the Knicks in five games to win the

**Chamberlain's will-
ingness to concen-
trate on rebounding
helped extend the
streak and keep the
Lakers on their way
to their first title in
Los Angeles.**

franchise's first championship since it
moved to Los Angeles in 1960.

The emotion in the Lakers locker room
was equal parts joy and relief. After all, this
was a team that had dropped four seventh
games in the NBA finals in the previous
decade. Now West had finally captured his
first title and Chamberlain his second. It was
more than a championship. It was a catharsis. "For a
long time my fans have had to put up with people saying that Wilt couldn't win the big ones," Chamberlain
said after securing the title. "Now maybe they'll have a
chance to walk in peace, like I do."

163

Pittsburgh rookie Frank Taveras once had the audacity to beat out a two-strike bunt against St. Louis pitcher Bob Gibson. During Taveras's next at-bat, Gibson drilled him in the back with a fastball, and while the batter was writhing in the dirt, Gibson walked over to him and barked, "Try to bunt that one, busher." It was a spring training game.

Another time Pete LaCock of the Cubs hit a home run off Gibson. The unhappy pitcher shadowed LaCock around the bases hurling epithets.

It's fair to say that Gibson hurled all of his pitches like epithets. On the mound Gibson was invariably angry. Dimestore psychologists have theorized that Gibson's temper stemmed from a poor, fatherless childhood during which he suffered from asthma that left him so tiny and sickly that he became the target of playground ridicule. More likely it was because Gibson astutely recognized that his wicked demeanor left most hitters behind in the count before they reached the batter's box. "He was a fierce competitor," says Gibson's teammate Mike Shannon, "not because he wanted to win, but because he despised losing."

Gibson was the tempestuous spark that drove the Cardinals throughout the 1960s, but try as he might he couldn't win games by himself. After Stan (The Man) Musial's retirement following the '63 season, St. Louis needed an offensive catalyst, which led general manager Bing Devine to take a huge gamble. In June of '64, Devine traded away 20-game winner Ernie Broglio in a deal for an unproven 25-year-old Cubs outfielder named Lou Brock, who had never hit higher than .263 in the majors. "I didn't think it was a good trade," Cardinals first baseman Bill White said. "We traded for a guy who didn't know how to play. If anybody tells you they approved of that trade, they're lying."

With White, second baseman Julian

In his quest to repeat in 1968, manager Red Schoendienst had a team loaded with stars at his disposal.

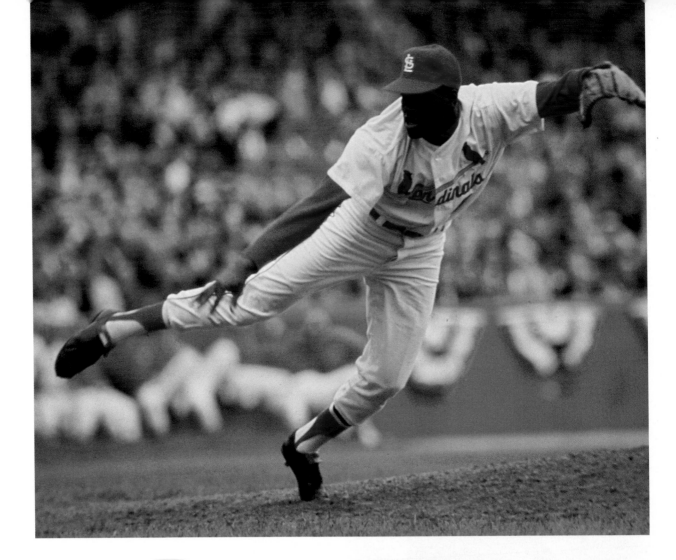

Spotlight

It took Lou Brock 13 steps to steal second—an unlucky number for catchers who were outrun by Brock 938 times during his 18-year career. Faced with his explosive speed, opposing teams would lose their rhythm and concentration. "They know I am going," he once said, "but they don't know when." Indeed, the tension and excitement this quiet math major out of Southern University in Louisiana brought to the game was palpable. At times he seemed to singlehandedly defeat opponents. Take the '67 World Series victory against Boston. He hit .414 over seven games, going four-for-four in Game 1 with a pair of steals. In the deciding game he stole three more bases. In his 21 World Series games, Brock batted .391, the highest ever for 20 or more contests; crossed the plate 16 times; and drove in 13 runs. Brock twice led the league in runs scored and wound up with 1,610 in his career. In his 16 seasons with the Cardinals, he hit his way into base-stealing position some 3,000 times. As he said, "If you can't hit, you don't get on base often enough to make a reputation as a base stealer."

In addition to the ferocious Gibson (far left) on the mound and the fleet Brock on the basepaths, the Cards were helped by outfielders Curt Flood (above) who hit .335 in 1967, and Roger Maris (below, left), who gave them a veteran presence in rightfield.

Javier, shortstop Dick Groat and third baseman Ken Boyer, the Cardinals already possessed what Branch Rickey called "the greatest hitting infield I have ever seen," but Brock added the element of speed. He stole 43 bases in '64 and hit .348 during his 103 games in a St. Louis uniform. Still, the Cardinals were 6½ games back with 12 left to play before the Philadelphia Phillies suffered the greatest collapse in pennant race history, losing 10 straight games down the stretch. St. Louis was virtually handed its first pennant in 18 years.

The '64 World Series against the Yankees shifted in favor of St. Louis when Boyer hit a grand slam in the sixth inning of Game 4, giving the Cardinals a 4–3 win. As Boyer rounded the bases, he passed his brother, Clete, the New York third baseman, who couldn't help muttering, "Attaboy." Gibson won Game 7 by pitching a complete game in the 7–5 victory.

The Cardinals muddled through disappointing seasons in '65 and '66, the only bright spot occurring when the team acquired Orlando Cepeda in a trade with the San Francisco Giants. Cepeda put together an MVP season in '67, hitting .325, with 25 homers and

111 RBI and Brock became the first player ever to hit 20 homers and steal 50 bases in the same season. When Gibson missed six weeks with a broken leg that season, the pitching staff was buoyed by a young southpaw named Steve Carlton, who won 14 games and helped secure the pennant. The Cardinals beat the Red Sox in seven games in the World Series as Brock batted .414 and stole a Series-record seven bases. Gibson pitched three more complete game victories.

That merely foreshadowed Gibson's excellence in '68, when he finished 22–9 with 13 shutouts and a microscopic 1.12 ERA, numbers that garnered him the Cy Young and league MVP awards. St. Louis easily won the '68 pennant, and in one of the most anticipated pitching matchups in World Series history, Gibson squared off against Detroit's 31-game winner, Denny McLain, in Game 1. Gibson threw a five-hit shutout and struck out a Series-record 17 Tigers. While Gibson would set yet another record by fanning 35 batters in the series, he lost Game 7 to Mickey Lolich, ending Gibson's unprecedented string of seven straight complete-game World Series victories in '64, '67 and '68. Another title run in '69 was not in the Cards, but Gibson's near-perfect season the year before did precipitate baseball's decision to lower the pitcher's mound by five inches. "Gibson was the luckiest pitcher ever," his catcher, Tim McCarver, has said. "Whenever he pitched, the other team didn't score."

29

Davis (right) collected a team of talented renegades to embody his outlaw philosophy, including the outspoken Stabler (opposite page), whose scrambling, free-throwing style suited the team perfectly.

Al Davis and his Raiders had just humbled Washington 38–9 in Super Bowl XVIII when Davis met with his sworn enemy, NFL commissioner Pete Rozelle, to accept the championship trophy for the second time in four seasons. Davis, the most notorious rebel owner in NFL history, clutched the hardware, smiled broadly in Rozelle's direction and said with a sneer, "Just win, baby."

The phrase was Davis's mantra, and his players listened and obeyed. During the first 20 years of Super Bowl competition the Raiders reached the AFL or AFC title game an amazing 11 times, more than any other team. The Raiders enjoyed 20 winning seasons in the 22 years from 1963 to '84, and they had a .715 winning percentage over that span, the best in all of pro sports.

The Raiders, who billed themselves as the Team of the Decades, maintained their enduring excellence with a revolving cast of malcontents who were somehow able to take out their vast frustrations on the guys in the enemy uniforms for three hours each Sunday. Davis's philosophy was to sign players who were motivated by failure with other

teams and bring them to his football rehab center, which became known as "Orphanage West." These bad boys of the NFL dressed in silver and black and looked even more ominous with the distinctive knife-wielding-pirate motif on their helmets. "We're not a bunch of choirboys and boy scouts," guard Gene Upshaw once said. "We're the halfway house of pro football and we live up to that image every chance we get."

The team's nasty attitude originated in the owner's box. Davis, an avid student of military history, insisted that the words, "Let's go to war!" be typed at the end of every Raiders itinerary. It was fitting that Davis's football doctrine was based on impenetrable defense and an offense that fired a barrage of bombs.

Still, despite the team's glowing victory percentage throughout the '60s and '70s, the Raiders often ended up as bridesmaids. They never captured a championship until the 1976 season, when the Raiders went 13–1 in the regular season and advanced to face Minnesota in Super Bowl XI. Oakland whipped the Vikings 32–14 using a diverse offense that featured customary lengthy passes from Ken Stabler to Fred Biletnikoff, complemented by Clarence Davis's 137 rushing yards. "They say we recruit from Central Park, that we're a bunch of thieves and cutthroats," Davis said after the victory. "I guess we've shut up the critics now."

In the 1980 season the Raiders won another title, led by quarterback Jim Plunkett, the 1970 Heisman Trophy winner whom Davis had rescued from the NFL scrap heap.

Plunkett won the Super Bowl XV Most Valuable Player award by throwing three touchdown passes and steering Oakland past the Philadelphia Eagles, 27–10. Another Davis reclamation project, linebacker Rod Martin, intercepted three passes to seal the victory.

In 1982 the owner who adored carpetbaggers became one himself, packing up his team and moving it from Oakland to Los Angeles against the express wishes of the NFL. The following season the renegade Los Angeles Raiders reached another title game and routed Washington by 29 points, the biggest blowout in any Super Bowl to

Biletnikoff, not fast but sneaky quick, was the Raiders' go-to guy, who consistently found a way to get open; in '76 he grabbed 43 passes for 551 yards and seven touchdowns.

that point. The victory marked the team's third championship in eight seasons.

The surprise star of that championship season was Todd Christensen, the ultimate poster boy for the Raider Nation. In 1978 Christensen had been drafted as a running back by the Dallas Cowboys, with whom he spent a year on injured reserve before being waived. The New York Giants picked him up and released him after one game. He then failed tryouts with the Green Bay Packers, New England Patriots, Chicago Bears and Philadelphia Eagles. Davis couldn't resist such a checkered past, so he invited Christensen to audition as a tight end. During the '83 season Christensen caught 92 passes, including 12 touchdown receptions, and then had four more catches in the title game. "After winning the Super Bowl my emotional income runneth over," Christensen said, "and I believe that the purpose of life is to maximize your emotional income."

It was Christensen's unique way of expressing a familiar mantra: "Just win, baby."

Mark Van Eeghen, one of the Raiders' overachievers, rushed for more than 1,000 yards in 1976, '77 and '78.

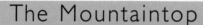

The Mountaintop

The Oakland Raiders toiled through an unusually long apprenticeship before becoming a championship franchise in the late 1970s and early '80s. After falling 33–14 to Green Bay in Super Bowl II, Oakland played in six of the next eight AFL or AFC title games and lost all six. When they finally broke through to the title game again, after the '76 season, their pairing with the Minnesota Vikings, losers of Super Bowls IV, VIII and IX, was couched as a battle of perennial chokers. One of the two would learn how to win the big game, how to breathe the rarefied air at championship altitude, the other would only enhance its reputation as a big-time loser.

The Vikings began well enough, blocking a Raiders punt and recovering on the Oakland three-yard line. Two plays later, however, they fumbled it right back, and the Raiders were on their way. Mixing passes to game MVP Fred Biletnikoff with punishing runs by Pete Banaszak, Oakland built a 19–0 lead en route to a 32–14 rout. The Raiders went on to two more Super Bowl victories in the '80s. Minnesota hasn't been back since.

1966 71   **Baltimore Orioles**

30

Still haunted by Baltimore's stunning loss to the Miracle Mets in the 1969 World Series, Brooks Robinson conjured up an idea early the next season to help exorcise his demons. He attached a tag to his luggage which read, BROOKS ROBINSON, 1970 WORLD CHAMPIONS.

Never in World Series history has a single player done more to fulfill such a daring prophecy. Robinson hit .429 in the '70 Series against the Reds, with two homers and six RBI. More important, he played the best defensive Fall Classic ever. The Orioles third baseman, who would earn 16 Gold Gloves in his Hall-of-Fame career, made no fewer than five brilliant plays at the hot corner during the five games. Twice he robbed Cincinnati's Lee May, who dubbed Robinson "The Human Vacuum Cleaner." Naturally, Robinson was named the Series MVP, and he was awarded a Dodge Charger, prompting Johnny Bench to say, "I'll bet it has an oversized glove compartment." After the World Series, Robinson's glove was sent to Cooperstown, where it remained until the following spring, when Robison reclaimed the miracle mitt because he could find no proper substitute.

The Orioles had initially ascended to championship heights with the arrival of another Robinson, Frank, in a Dec. 9, 1965 trade with the Reds. Frank homered in his first Orioles at-bat, in spring training, and he won the Triple Crown in '66 by leading the American League in batting (.316), homers (49) and RBI (122)—sterling stats which earned him an MVP award. On May 6 against Luis Tiant, Robinson became the only player ever to hit a ball completely out of Memorial Stadium. Orioles pitchers stole the spotlight in the World Series, setting a record by blanking the Dodgers over the last 33

Orioles reliever Moe Drabowsky received congratulations from Robinson (left) and Johnson (15) after hurling 6⅔ scoreless innings to win Game 1 of the '66 Series.

The fiery Weaver (left) got great production from **Palmer**, who pitched a complete-game shutout in the second game of the '66 Series (above), and **Brooks Robinson** (above right), who made the '70 Series his personal showcase.

innings. Jim Palmer, Wally Bunker and Dave McNally threw shutouts in Games 2, 3 and 4 to clinch the series.

The Orioles struggled mightily in '67 and again in '68, leading the front office to hire a tempestuous new manager, Earl Weaver, who swiftly laid out his keys to success: good pitching; solid defense; timely three-run homers.

Baltimore supplied Weaver with plenty of all three in 1969. McNally and Mike Cuellar both won 20 games. Brooks Robinson, Mark Belanger, Davey Johnson and Paul Blair each won Gold Gloves. Four Orioles cracked 20 homers, led by Boog Powell, who had 37. With Weaver cracking the whip, Baltimore won 109 games, just two short of the American League record set by the '54 Indians, and then swept the Minnesota Twins in the first-ever American League Championship Series to earn the right to face the overachieving Mets. After Baltimore won Game 1, the Mets' pitching took over, beating the best team in baseball in four straight games.

Early in 1970 an opposing player snidely commented that the Orioles were not supermen, provoking Robinson, Blair and others to begin wearing Superman T-shirts under their jerseys. Baltimore won 108 games in the regular season, and seven Ori-

oles made the American League All-Star team, including Powell, who hit 35 homers and won the MVP. McNally, Cuellar and Palmer all were 20-game winners. Baltimore swept the Twins again in the ALCS and then smothered Cincinnati, with the help of Robinson's golden glove.

In 1971, McNally, Cuellar, Palmer and newcomer Pat Dobson each won at least 20 games—becoming the first foursome to do so since Red Farber, Lefty Williams, Eddie Cicotte, Dickie Kerr did for the White Sox in 1920. Once again the Orioles swept the ALCS, with three wins over Oakland, only to lose the World Series to the Pirates in seven games, during which the Orioles' offense batted .205 and their vaunted defense committed nine errors.

Still, in six seasons, Baltimore had played in four World Series, capturing two championships, and suddenly everybody wanted to know what Brooks Robinson was scribbling on his luggage tags.

Spotlight

Cornerstones of the Baltimore Orioles dynasty of the late 1960s and early '70s, Frank Robinson and Brooks Robinson (no relation), entered the Baseball Hall of Fame in 1982 and '83, respectively. Frank is the only man ever to win MVP awards in both the National and American Leagues (Cincinnati '61, Baltimore '66). Brooks won 16 consecutive Gold Gloves while minding third base like a goalie for Baltimore, where he spent his entire 23-year career. Though Brooks was an Orioles lifer, Frank's No. 20 was the first Baltimore uniform to be retired, going behind glass in 1972. Frank's 586 career home runs place him fourth on the alltime list. Brooks is the alltime leader among third basemen in putouts, assists, chances and double plays. Frank became the first African-American manager in both the AL and the NL (Cleveland Indians and San Francisco Giants), and won Manager of the Year awards in both leagues.

Photography Credits

Front Cover   Hardcover edition: John Biever.
Softcover edition: bottom, John Biever;
top left, Neil Leifer; top right, John W.
McDonough.

Back Cover   Brown Brothers.

Front Matter   Half-title page, Herb Scharfman;
Title page, Sam Forencich.

Introduction   6, Hy Peskin; 7, David E. Klutho;
8, John D. Hanlon; 9, Jerry Wachter.

Dynasties

10–11, Associated Press; 12, Associated Press; 13, Brown Brothers; 14, top, Ray Matjasic/Cleveland Plain-Dealer, bottom, Richard Mackson; 15, Neil Leifer; 16, UPI/Corbis-Bettmann; 17, UPI/Corbis-Bettmann; 18, UPI/Corbis-Bettmann; 19, UPI/Corbis-Bettmann; 20, Greg Viller/Life; 21, top, UPI/Corbis-Bettmann, bottom, Arthur Rickerby/Life; 22, Neil Leifer; 23, Ronald C. Modra; 24, Lane Stewart; 25, Walter Iooss Jr.; 26, Walter Iooss Jr.; 27, Walter Iooss Jr.; 28, Walter Iooss Jr.; 30, Manny Millan; 31, George Tiedemann; 33, Tony Triolo; 34, UPI/Corbis-Bettmann; 35, John G. Zimmerman; 36, Tony Triolo; 37, James Drake; 38, left, Tony Triolo, right, Manny Millan; 39, David E. Klutho.

Teams of a Decade

40–41, Marvin E. Newman; 42, Neil Leifer; 44, Tony Triolo; 45, Walter Iooss Jr.; 46, Neil Leifer; 48, Walter Iooss Jr.; 49, Walter Iooss Jr.; 50, John Iacono; 51, Peter Read Miller; 52, Bill Frakes; 54, John W. McDonough; 55, John W. McDonough; 56, left, Al Tielemans; right, Manny Millan; 57, Andrew D. Bernstein/NBA Photos; 59, Walter Iooss Jr.; 61, Neil Leifer; 62, Walter Iooss Jr.; 63, Walter Ioos Jr.; 64, Herb Scharfman; 65, James Drake; 66, Manny Millan; 67, Walter Iooss Jr; 68, Heinz Kluetmeier; 69, John Iacono; 70, Heinz Kluetmeier; 72, Walter Iooss Jr.; 73, Jerry Wachter; 74, Peter Read Miller; 75, top, John W. McDonough, bottom, Any Hayt; 76, Peter Read Miller; 77, Richard Mackson; 78, Richard Mackson; 79, Rich Clarkson; 80, Peter Read Miller; 81, Richard Mackson; 82, Paul J. Bereswill; 84, Paul J. Bereswill; 85, David E. Klutho; 86, Heinz Kluetmeier; 87, Paul J. Bereswill; 88, Hy Peskin; 90, Associated Press; 91, Ray Matjasic/Cleveland Plain-Dealer; 92, UPI/Corbis-Bettmann; 94, left, UPI/Corbis-Bettmann, right, David Peskin/Life; 95, UPI/Corbis-Bettmann; 96, UPI/Corbis-Bettmann; 98, Imperial Oil-Turofsky/Hockey Hall of Fame; 99, Imperial Oil-Turofsky/Hockey Hall of Fame.

Also Greats

100–101, Chuck Solomon; 103, Walter Iooss Jr.; 104, James Drake; 105, Neil Leifer; 106, Walter Iooss Jr.; 108, left, Herb Scharfman, right, Herb Scharfman; 109, Tony Triolo; 111, John Iacono; 112, Anthony Neste; 113, Anthony Neste; 115, Walter Iooss Jr.; 116, top, Neil Leifer, bottom, Neil Leifer; 117, Fred Kaplan/Black Star; 118, Howard Sochurek/Life; 120, UPI/Corbis-Bettmann; 121, Imperial Oil-Turofsky/Hockey Hall of Fame; 122, Peter Read Miller; 123, Peter Read Miller; 124, Robert Beck; 125, Peter Read Miller; 136, Brown Brothers; 128, Brown Brothers; 129, UPI/Corbis-Bettmann; 130, UPI/Corbis-Bettmann; 132, Brown Brothers; 133, Associated Press; 134, George Silk/Life; 135, Francis Miller/Life; 136, left, Ralph Morse/Life, right, George Silk/Life; 137, John Dominis/Life; 138, Walter Iooss Jr.; 139, Dick Raphael; 140, left, Lane Stewart, right, Walter Iooss Jr.; 141, Walter Iooss Jr.; 143, Associated Press; 144, left, UPI/Corbis-Bettmann, right, National Baseball Library; 145, UPI/Corbis-Bettmann; 147, Walter Bennett/Time magazine; 148, Walter Bennett/Time Magazine; 149, Associated Press; 150, Walter Iooss Jr.; 151, Neil Leifer; 153, Coe Rentmeester/Life; 155, Ronald C. Modra; 156, Ronald C. Modra; 157, Martha Jane Stanton; 159, James Drake; 160, Sheedy & Long; 161, James Drake; 162, Neil Leifer; 164, top, Walter Iooss Jr., bottom, Bob Peterson; 165, Herb Scharfman; 166, Peter Read Miller; 167, Neil Leifer; 168, Walter Iooss Jr.; 169, James Drake; 170, Neil Leifer; 172, top, Neil Leifer, bottom, Tony Triolo; 173, Herb Scharfman.

Index